Learn *Small Business* ACCOUNTING in 7 DAYS

BLITZ YOUR PAYROLL

ROD CALDWELL

Wrightbooks

For my darling wife Robyn, without whose support and encouragement this book would never have been written.

First published 2011 by Wrightbooks
an imprint of John Wiley & Sons Australia, Ltd
42 McDougall Street, Milton Qld 4064

Office also in Melbourne

Typeset in 11.3/14 pt Berkeley LT

© Rod Caldwell 2011

The moral rights of the author have been asserted

National Library of Australia Cataloguing-in-Publication data:

Author:	Caldwell, Rod.
Title:	Learn small business accounting in 7 days / Rod Caldwell.
ISBN:	9780730376798 (pbk.)
Notes:	Includes index.
Subjects:	Small business—Accounting.
Dewey number:	657.9042

Cover design by Xou Creative

Tables 2.7 and 3.5 and Figures 6.1, 6.2, 6.3, 6.6, 7.1, 7.2, 7.3, 7.4 and 7.6 © Australian Taxation Office. The ATO material included in this publication was current at the time of publishing. Readers should refer to the ATO website <www.ato.gov.au> for up-to-date ATO information.

Printed in Australia by Ligare Book Printer

10 9 8 7 6 5 4 3 2 1

Disclaimer
The material in this publication is of the nature of general comment only, and does not represent professional advice. It is not intended to provide specific guidance for particular circumstances and it should not be relied on as the basis for any decision to take action or not take action on any matter which it covers. Readers should obtain professional advice where appropriate, before making any such decision. To the maximum extent permitted by law, the author and publisher disclaim all responsibility and liability to any person, arising directly or indirectly from any person taking or not taking action based upon the information in this publication.

Contents

About the author

Rod Caldwell is a tax accountant by profession and a TAFE business lecturer by choice. He worked for the Australian Taxation Office (ATO) for 20 years before leaving in 2005 to start a new career as a lecturer in business studies at a Perth technical college. Rod has a bachelor of commerce degree from the University of Western Australia and a postgraduate diploma in advanced taxation from the University of New South Wales. Rod is also a Fellow of CPA Australia.

This book was written as a direct result of his involvement with small business owners through the Adult and Community Education courses he delivers in Western Australia. Rod is also the author of *Learn Bookkeeping in 7 Days*.

Additional resources are available from the author's website <www.tpabusiness.com.au>. The author can be contacted by email at <rod@tpabusiness.com.au>. All comments from the readers of this book, students or lecturers are welcome.

Preface

Who should read this book?

Learn Small Business Accounting in 7 Days is aimed at the small business operator, often a home-based business, with an annual turnover of less than $2 million, as well as larger businesses with a turnover of up to $20 million. It is the second book in the Learn in 7 Days series, the first being *Learn Bookkeeping in 7 Days*.

This book assumes that the reader is aware of bookkeeping procedures to a standard at least equal to that covered in *Learn Bookkeeping in 7 Days*. It takes the reader from the trial balance stage, where we were at the end of *Learn Bookkeeping in 7 Days,* to the production of the final accounting reports. The book also covers payroll.

This book as a lecturer's resource

If you are considering using this text for a non-accredited course in accounting, your course is probably a series of two- or three-hour sessions over six to eight weeks. This text has been deliberately constructed over seven evenly deliverable 'days' in order to facilitate this.

Resources for lecturers' use, such as additional exercises and the exercise solutions, are available from my website at <www.tpabusiness.com.au>.

Rod Caldwell
Perth
May 2011

Day 1

Setting the scene

Key terms and concepts

- ▶ *International Financial Reporting Standards (IFRS):* a legally enforceable set of accounting standards that apply to larger businesses.

- ▶ *Generally Accepted Accounting Practices (GAAP):* a set of standards that apply on a voluntary basis to all entities.

- ▶ *Small to medium enterprises (SME):* business entities that usually fall within the $20 million to $100 million turnover that are subject to IFRS.

- ▶ *Small business entity:* a tax term for a business with a turnover of less than $2 million.

- ▶ *Small business:* the generally accepted term for businesses with a turnover between $2 million and $20 million and fewer than five employees.

- ▶ *Micro business:* the term that usually refers to businesses with a turnover less than $2 million that do not employ any staff.

▶ *Sole proprietor:* a person in business by themselves with no formal structure.

▶ *Partnership:* two people, usually a husband and wife, working together in the business.

▶ *Company:* a formally registered proprietary limited entity that is legally separate from the owners.

▶ *Trust:* a tax effective method of running a business that combines elements of a partnership and a company.

We are at war!

As a **small business** proprietor, have you ever tried to find the answer to a very simple question, only to be bombarded by an avalanche of extraneous material? You wade through this material hoping that your answer may be there somewhere, only to be cut down time and again. Finally you just give up.

The information revolution, which started with so much promise, has degenerated into an electronic information war. We are bombarded by volumes of material, only a fraction of which is relevant to us. The prime cause of this is twofold: the cost restraints of a paper-based information society are being replaced by the 'no cost' electronic equivalent, and also because of the underlying perception that 'more is better'.

The **Australian Taxation Office (ATO)** is one of the prime culprits. Why say something meaningful in 20 words when you can now use 200 or 2000 for the same cost and appear to be all the more knowledgeable for it? The Tax Office appears to have little understanding of the needs of its readers and is 'silo' driven. By this, I mean that the Tax Office consists of public servants all serving a different master. The **GST** 'silo' will only comment on GST matters, even when what they are commenting about has an impact on other areas. For this reason you have to hunt the database for the complete answer, rather than your question being anticipated and the answer readily available to you.

This book is a shield

This book deals only with the main issues, the issues that you deal with most of the time. It reduces the information bombardment into manageable units that you can easily understand and presents you with workable solutions in an easy-to-read, easy-to-digest format.

What is covered in this book?

This book assumes that you already have a background in **bookkeeping**. You understand the difference between a **debit** and a **credit**, what a **transaction** is and you are familiar with **journals**, ledgers and the **trial balance**. We start at the trial balance stage and move forward, through end-of-period adjustments to the **final reports**. On the way we look at **assets** and **inventory**, then some speciality subjects such as the employment and remuneration of staff members.

But this is first and foremost an **accounting** text. We look at the financial aspects of business management and what drives it, but we will not be looking at how to run a business.

What influences financial decisions?

Why are we in business? The simplistic answer is often 'to make money!' But this is not usually the prime driving force behind small business owners. People start small businesses for many reasons:

▶ *Accidental businesses.* This type of small business is best explained by example. An accountant retires and starts to make wooden toys for his grandchildren. In order to finance his hobby he also sells his toys at a market stall. So far his activity could be called a hobby. However, a toy store sees his product and asks if he could supply the store with a few samples to 'see how it goes'. The hobby is now a business.

▶ *Contractors*. Many tradespeople are in business as contractors rather than **wage** employees. Many professionals in the accounting and IT industries are also becoming contractors. This is usually a lifestyle choice.

▶ *Home based*. Home-based businesses—in particular, internet-based sales businesses—are a growing trend. These businesses are often started by stay-at-home mums to supplement the family income. Often home-based businesses grow into a fully fledged business enterprise in their own right. The downside can be the feeling of isolation that being at home 24/7 brings.

▶ *Lifestyle*. 'Wouldn't it be nice if...?' is the question that all salaried and wage employees have asked themselves more than once. But the reality is often less than they expected: long hours for small returns are the norm.

Business planning is the traditional approach to formally starting a small business and many small businesses are started with the intention of achieving goals. If, however, you are already in business it is not too late to think about where you are going and what you really wish to achieve.

Business planning is the key to success and should not be underestimated. It is not a single exercise to be done and put into the bottom drawer. Business planning is a continual cycle of planning, budgeting, analysing performance, then modifying and remodifying your goals.

Who wants to know?

Your money-making efforts will attract the notice of a number of interested parties. The Tax Office will be deeply interested in your efforts, not only from the viewpoint of the money you make, but also from the perspective of the GST you collect and pay, and income that you pay to your staff. Other interested parties include your bank, which wants to know if you are making sufficient funds to cover your loans, and your investors. You may not have any investors yet, but what about when it comes time to either grow or sell your business? You will need to present a full set of books for the last three years in order to maximise your return.

Your financial affairs are regulated by Generally Accepted Accounting Principles (GAAP), a voluntary code developed by accounting societies to encourage consistency in reporting. However, as a result of a number of spectacular failures of companies whose financial reports were less than perfect, governments worldwide are now adopting and legislating **International Financial Reporting Standards (IFRS)**.

The IFRS standards are law in Australia and regulated through the Australian Accounting Standards Board (AASB). They apply to any reporting entity (the GAAP still applies, voluntarily, to all others). A reporting entity is any entity that has external stakeholders and therefore can apply to companies with **turnovers** as low as $20 million (**small to medium enterprises** or SMEs). We limit our discussion to entities that have no external stakeholders, or shareholders, and have a turnover less than $20 million. However, GAAP is slowly being replaced by IFRS standards and therefore it makes sense to apply IFRS wherever possible, even if we are not legally obliged to do so.

Another reason to adopt IFRS is that government entities are now slowly adopting IFRS principles in their reporting requirements and this includes tax law. The tax provisions on FOREX (foreign exchange) specifically mention IFRS and apply different reporting requirements to IFRS-compliant entities than they do to others.

The good news is that on a practical level for small businesses, tax law requirements and the requirements of GAAP and IFRS are rarely at odds. The main thrust of IFRS is to address the very complex transactions of large business corporations where the various GAAPs varied in their treatment.

What is a small business?

This book is aimed at small businesses with turnover of less than $20 million, which covers two business sectors, the micro sector with a turnover up to $2 million and small business up to $20 million. For the purposes of the discussion on payroll we assume you have fewer than 10 employees.

This may appear a strange distinction to some readers because the Tax Office defines a small business as a business entity with a turnover of less than $2 million, while the Australian Bureau of Statistics (ABS) uses employee numbers and IFRS defines a small to medium enterprise (SME) in terms that could include a $100 million entity.

There are many definitions of small and medium business. In this book we use the following definitions.

▶ A *micro business* is a business entity with a turnover of up to $2 million that satisfies the tax office definition of a small business and is able to use small business tax concessions. These are often home-based businesses.

▶ A *small business* is a business with a turnover of more than $2 million that is not able to use the small business tax concession but does not have any external investors; that is, it does not fall within the IFRS definition of an SME.

▶ A *small to medium enterprise* is a reporting entity for IFRS purposes; that is, it has external investors who are not part of the internal management team of the entity.

This book covers the accounting requirements of both micro and small businesses and relies heavily on the tax office requirements for this purpose. The reasoning behind this is that a **micro business** will often grow very quickly into a **small business entity**. A plumber will often start off as a micro business, then employ an apprentice who becomes the first employee and so the entity grows.

There are millions of small and micro businesses in Australia. Of the 2 051 085 actively **trading businesses** in Australia in June 2009, more than 95 per cent were small (employing fewer than 20 people, the majority less than five). Two-thirds of these small businesses do not employ any staff and are considered to be micro businesses. Only 1 per cent of businesses employ more than 20 staff. More than 65 per cent of businesses had a turnover of less than $2 million.

Small business tax concessions

If you are in business, irrespective of the legal type of business you have, and the total turnover of all your business activities is less than $2 million, either actual or estimated, then you are able to use the small business tax concessions. These concessions are:

▶ simplified **depreciation** rules that we discuss on day 2 when we look at assets

▶ simplified trading **stock** rules that we look at on day 3 when we discuss inventory

▶ immediate deduction for prepaid expenses that we discuss on day 4 when we look at end-of-year adjustments and the final reports.

However, the main concession is that we can report our income tax obligation under **cash accounting** rules and if we do this we can also report our GST obligations on our BAS under cash accounting rules.

Cash versus accrual

If you are dealing strictly in **cash** then this section does not really apply to you, but if you either purchase inventory or sell your services or inventory on a credit (pay later) basis, then this is certainly of concern. Under accounting rules you record the purchase or sale at the time that all of the legally enforceable conditions of the contract have been complied with; that is, at the time you become the owner of the goods, or supply the goods and services. The question of the exact time that 'property' in inventory transfers to someone else is discussed in day 3, which is devoted to inventory issues.

The problem we face is that, if you record your **purchases** and sales at the time of the transaction and not at the time of receipt of payment, then you have to pay both your income tax obligations and your GST obligations in real cash, possibly before your clients settle their accounts. This can lead to cash flow issues.

The good news for micro businesses (small business entities according to the Tax Office definition) is that irrespective of how you conduct the transaction, you only account to the Tax Office for income tax and GST when payment is received. However, this applies only to **revenue** items. You can still claim your full GST credit on assets bought on time payment terms.

A side benefit of accounting for your transaction when you receive the cash is that if one of your clients goes 'bad', then you do not have to make income tax and GST adjustments for

bad debts, as the income amount was not reported in the first instance.

A problem with accounting on a cash basis occurs when you move from a micro to a small business. Small businesses with a turnover of more than $2 million must account for their transactions on an accrual basis. But some of your accrual transactions will not have been reported under your previous cash regime and therefore you will be required to make an adjustment for GST and income tax, which is almost akin to a penalty for growing beyond the micro stage.

Small business structures

According to the ABS, at June 2009 there were 605015 sole proprietors, 360228 partnerships, 414020 trusts and 670951 companies in Australia. Let's take a look at the difference between each type of entity.

Sole proprietorship

When you first start out in business it is usually just you alone. Legally you are the business—you are responsible for all of the debts of the business and entitled to all of the profits. The business cheque account holds the funds that you have allocated to the business and over which you have full control. However, under the entity convention the business funds belong to the business and you, as the business owner, are treated as a completely separate entity. The entity convention is the cornerstone of accounting principles and that applies equally to all **legal entity** types.

You must account for your business funds separately from your private funds. Your business funds and private funds must be kept and treated as two distinctly separate amounts. When you pay for private expenditure out of business funds you must record this in your business accounts.

Partnership

The most tax effective way to minimise your tax bill is to split your income with your spouse. The easiest way to do this is to go into **partnership**. This means that your spouse will have an equal say over how the business operates, but is also equally liable for any debts and entitled to any profits that the business may make. The presumption of a 50–50 split can be modified by agreement, called a **partnership agreement**, but usually in the husband-and-wife situation the most cost effective method is to have the business funds held in joint names as proof of the existence of the partnership. No other legal formalities are required.

However, if you are going into partnership with anyone other than your spouse, you should seek legal advice and have a formal partnership agreement drawn up. The reason for this is the legal term 'joint and several', which means that you are not just responsible for your portion of the debts, but in fact all of the partners are all 100 per cent responsible for all of the debts of the business.

Family trust

If the idea of a partnership with your spouse does not appeal to you but you still wish to take advantage of the tax relief obtained by splitting your income for tax purposes, then a trust is the best method to use. Under a trust you can also include other members of your family who will share the tax burden, but not have any say in, or control over, the running of the business.

A family trust is the most common form of trust, where all of the beneficiaries are members of your immediate family. This legal structure would normally be set up by your accountant and requires the creation of a trust deed.

For accounting purposes, the cheque account is the business and your legal arrangements only come into play in the distribution of the profits (taxable income) of the business. As the sole owner of the business, you are still responsible for all of the business debts but none of the profits as these now belong to the beneficiaries.

Companies

Very few small businesses run through a traditional **company** structure. This is because you are limited to a small number of shareholders and therefore your source of finance is also limited and the distribution of profits is a rather difficult exercise. The positive side is that under the company rules you are limited in your liability to the amount of funds you have invested in the business. This is why small business owners are often confronted with personal guarantees that banks and other creditors will insist upon to override this protection.

Now we get complicated!

A lot of businesses are owned by companies, but the companies are being used as a shield and a conduit for the distribution of profits to non-participating family members. A trust, even a family trust, must have a trustee in charge, who owns and runs the business. However, a business is a legal entity, able to transact on its own account through its agents (owners). Therefore the trustee of a family trust can be a single director, single shareholder company.

In effect you can have it both ways. As the single director of a company that owns the business, all debts of the business are limited to your shareholding, usually $1. The company, acting through its agent (which in this case is you), can decide who in the family will get which part of the business income so that you minimise your tax bill. This type of structure is known as a corporate trustee of a discretionary family trust.

Although this structure is by far the most common for tax purposes, it is also the most expensive to run. A small business accountant's bill of between $5000 and $10 000 per year would not be unusual. The easiest way to keep this bill under control is to make sure that your accounts are kept correctly in the first instance and that your accountant has as little bookkeeping to do as possible, which is the objective of this book.

Chart of accounts revisited

From your knowledge of bookkeeping you will know that a **chart of accounts** acts as an index to the **general ledger**. There is no formal structure to a chart of accounts; it can be laid out in any manner that you see fit. However, for this text we will use what has become known as the standard chart of accounts as is commonly used in most small business accounting programs such as MYOB and Quicken.

A general ledger is divided into categories (or sections), usually assets, liabilities, equity, revenue, **cost of sales** and expenses. Under the standard chart of accounts we allocate the numbers 1 to 6 to each of these sections:

1   Assets

2   Liabilities

3   Equity

4   Revenue

5   Cost of sales

6   Expenses.

However, the revenue, cost of sales and expenses categories contain only income and expense items that relate to the operations of the business. For income and expenses outside normal trading operations we need two further categories:

8   Other income

9   Other expenses.

Item 7 is not used to comply with the MYOB standard chart of accounts.

Assets

An asset is an outlay that will provide a future benefit, such as the purchase of a motor vehicle. Many assets, for example property, plant and equipment, have a physical form. However, physical form is not essential to the existence of an asset. Patents and copyrights, for example, are assets if they have a future economic benefit that is expected to benefit the business.

Assets are further subdivided into three categories:

▶ current assets

▶ noncurrent assets

▶ intangible assets.

A **current asset** provides a future benefit within the next accounting cycle. Current assets are typically liquid assets such as cash and **accounts receivable**.

A noncurrent asset will provide a future benefit over a longer term and was previously known as a fixed asset. Most physical assets such as PPE (property, plant and equipment) are **noncurrent assets**. The cost of a noncurrent asset, with the exception of land, is usually allocated to an expense over its effective life by a process known as depreciation.

Intangible assets are assets with no physical form, such as patents and copyrights. The **accounting standards** include intangible assets with noncurrent assets, but it is Australian practice to separate the two due to the difference in tax treatment. The cost of an intangible asset is usually allocated to an expense over its life by a process known as amortisation. Goodwill is an intangible asset that, under Australian Standards and tax law, is not amortised.

Assets are recorded in the accounts at their cost. This is known as the historical cost convention. They are recorded at the time that the 'property' in the assets passes. Property is a legal term that represents a bundle of rights, the most significant of which is the right to dispose of the asset as you see fit. If you can't sell it you don't own it!

Each year you review the holding cost of your assets in a process known as an impairment review to see if they are still worth at least their carrying value. Assets and asset valuations are discussed further in day 3.

Liabilities

An essential characteristic of a liability is that the entity has a present obligation that will result in a future outlay. You have a present obligation to pay for the goods and that obligation has been delayed to a future time under the conditions of the purchase. This can arise in the normal course of business where you purchase goods on credit terms.

Liabilities are divided into two categories:

▶ current liabilities

▶ noncurrent liabilities.

A current liability is required to be satisfied within the next accounting cycle. **Trade debtors** or loans of less than 12 months are two examples of **current liabilities**.

Noncurrent liabilities will be satisfied in the longer term. A mortgage is an example of a noncurrent liability.

The GST accounts, both as obligations and as credits, are usually categorised as liability accounts because they represent a net liability to the Tax Office. These accounts are only transient and are satisfied on a regular basis, so this is not seen as a problem unless the entity usually obtains a GST refund, in which case the account would be reclassified within the asset accounts. Classifying the GST accounts as either a current liability or as a third liability type would both be acceptable, although the classification as a current liability is preferable because the net effect is that the GST balance is a credit that represents your liability to the Tax Office for that period.

Equity or proprietorship

This is our third account type and contains the details of the owner's investment within the entity (usually referred to as the **capital** accounts) and the current profit position (referred to as retained earnings or reserves). Each of the separate business structure types—sole proprietor, partnership, company or trust—has a different equity accounts structure to account for the owner's contributions and **drawings** in anticipation of profits.

Revenue or income

The accounting standards definition of income concentrates on the receipts side, defining it as the increase in the value of an asset, usually either **cash at bank (CAB)** or accounts receivable.

I prefer to look at the entry in its own right as the counterside to the increase in the asset; that is, the outflow of economic value of the good sold or the service provided. Therefore I prefer the term revenue over income.

The revenue classification is used to hold the sales, fees, commissions or any other revenue-raising activity undertaken by the entity. It also holds the amounts that are directly negative to this, such as the discounts allowed. Revenue does not account for any amount not 'received' in the normal course of trade, such as the profit on the disposal of an asset or of interest received on the investment of surplus cash.

Revenue can only be recognised when it is actually earned or, as the accounting standards state, when the increase in the asset or reduction in the liability can be recorded. Work done that does not create a legally enforceable obligation is not income.

Cost of sales

This section is also known as the cost of goods sold although this is not strictly correct. In this section you will find all of the accounts that hold the purchase value and discounts received in relation to our inventory. The movement of inventory over the year is also accounted for under either a perpetual or a periodic system.

When combined with the revenue items these accounts form the basis of the trading account and determine the gross or trading profit and the mark up on sale. This rather extensive classification will be looked at in depth in day 4.

The cost of sales is included in the general term 'expenses' in the accounting standards and is therefore included in the same chart of accounts classification by some entities and organisations. I do not believe that this is the correct method of classification as the cost of sales is very specific to revenue in calculating the gross or trading profit.

Expenses

These accounts hold the everyday expenses of the business. They do not account for the abnormal or unusual expenses such as a loss on the sale of an asset. These are discussed in the section 'Other income and expenses'.

An expense is an outlay on something that is consumed, or will be consumed in the near future. It is recognised when the expenditure produces no future economic benefits or when the future economic benefit does not qualify for recognition in the **balance sheet** as an asset. But it is only recognised when the corresponding asset or liability is credited; that is, when there is a legal obligation to pay.

Some expenses are paid into the future, such as insurance. Only the amount that relates to this year is accounted for as an expense; the part that is a future economic benefit for future years is classified as an asset (a prepayment). This is discussed further in day 4.

Other income and expenses

The categories of revenue, cost of sales and expenses only hold accounts in relation to the day-to-day trading activities of the business. All unusual, uncommon or unplanned amounts should be included in the 'Other' categories.

Examples of other income include:

▶ profit on sale of an asset

▶ interest received from investments (interest paid is a normal expense)

▶ refund of income tax paid.

Examples of other expenses include:

▶ loss on sale of an asset

▶ income tax paid.

It should be noted that under the accounting standards these items should be shown with the trading income and expenses, not as abnormal items. This does not stop such items being shown in their own right at the bottom of the **income statement** (statement of financial performance). It just prevents misuse of the term 'abnormal'.

It is very important that the 'Other' items should be separately identified because your budget calculations and variances are all based on normal trading activity and not incidental occurrences.

Accounting conventions and doctrines

Accounting has been around for thousands of years but it wasn't until the 1500s that it was written down in the form of a textbook. The methodology was then introduced to the world through the expansion of the European empires, mainly in the 1800s. In each new territory a society of accountants was formed and they all started to make general rules to be followed by their members. These rules became known as the Generally Accepted Accounting Principles or GAAP.

By the mid 1980s the concept of the global village made this individual approach unworkable and all nations agreed to adhere to one international set of standards. These became known as the International Financial Reporting Standards (IFRS). The United States is one of the last to fully adopt these standards and is currently conducting an exercise to match its own version of GAAP with IFRS. Australia, through the Australian Accounting Standards Board (AASB), has been under the IFRS regime for a number of years.

Conventions and doctrines developed under the various GAAPs have been included in the accounting standards issued by the AASB and are therefore now law.

Under IFRS businesses are required to produce three general purpose reports:

▶ statement of financial position (usually known as the balance sheet)

▶ statement of financial performance (usually known as the income statement)

▶ statement of cash flows.

We look at the statement of financial position and the statement of financial performance on day 4.

These statements must be produced under the following assumptions:

▶ accrual basis

▶ going concern basis.

It is just as well that the IFRS pronouncements do not legally apply to small businesses, even though it is good practice to apply them where possible. If you have a turnover of less than $2 million you can account on a cash basis. IFRS requires that you account on an accrual basis, which requires two sets of books—one for the tax man and one for general reporting. Fortunately, with a little forethought you can keep just one set of books for all purposes.

Apart from the accrual basis, the other assumption is that your business is going to carry on and that you are not planning to go out of business. The values of business assets vary markedly between an ongoing business and one that is closing shop.

The statement of financial position and the statement of financial performance are also produced under the following qualitative characteristics:

- ▶ understandability
- ▶ relevance
- ▶ materality
- ▶ reliability
- ▶ faithful representation
- ▶ substance over form
- ▶ neutrality
- ▶ prudence
- ▶ completeness.

Financial statements should show a true and fair view of the financial position and performance of an entity. The application of the principal qualitative characteristics and of appropriate accounting standards normally results in financial statements that convey what is generally understood as a true and fair view of such information. However, in practice a balancing or trade-off between qualitative characteristics is often necessary. Generally, the aim is to achieve an appropriate balance among the characteristics in order to meet the objective of financial statements.

All the other qualitative requirements are really aimed at making you report your affairs as they truly are, not as you would like them to be or what they may appear to be. Many of these qualitative requirements are discussed in the following days.

Day 2

Assets, depreciation and registers

Key terms and concepts

▶ *Asset:* an item you (the business) purchase that is of future benefit to the business.

▶ *Materiality limit:* $1000 for a small business entity using the simplified depreciation rules; $300 for all other businesses.

▶ *Small business entity:* a business with a turnover of less than $2 million that wishes to be classified as a small business entity for taxation purposes.

▶ *Simplified depreciation rules:* special tax concessions for small business entities with a turnover of less than $2 million.

▶ *Uniform capital allowances (UCA):* the depreciation rules used by the Tax Office.

▶ *Effective life:* the useful life of an asset under normal operating conditions.

▶ *Depreciation:* the amount of an asset's cost that can be transferred to an expense each year.

▶ *Write off:* the process of transferring an asset's cost to an expense over its effective life.

▶ *Closing value:* the cost of an asset less its accumulated depreciation to date. Also known as *written down value*, *adjustable value* and *carrying value*.

What is an asset?

When you acquire an item that has a future benefit to the business you have acquired an asset.

▶ *You acquire:* you either purchase the item for cash or on credit terms, but it is something that you own, rather than something that you just rent or lease.

▶ *An item:* assets can be in the usual form of a physical good such as a motor vehicle, or in an intangible form such as a copyright, patent or goodwill.

▶ *Future benefit:* as distinct from a payment for a consumable such as rent, or something that will be consumed within the current accounting cycle such as insurance. Adjustments for expenses that cross the accounting year end are discussed in day 4.

Therefore when we purchase a good, be it in a tangible form or not, if it is something that is to be consumed then it is classified as an expense. However, if it is something durable and of future benefit to the business, then it is an asset. So the question now is, how do we correctly account for assets and expenses?

An expense is something that you allocate to an expense account and then write off to your profit and loss account. An asset on the other hand is allocated to a balance sheet account and is slowly written off to an expense over its useful life. This process is called either depreciation or amortisation and applies to most assets. Therefore an asset takes considerably more work to correctly account for compared with an expense.

Examples of assets include land, property, plant and equipment (PPE), office furniture and equipment, motor vehicles, warehouse fittings (such as shelving) as well as the intangible assets mentioned earlier. Examples of expenses include rent, electricity, wages, insurance, registration, servicing costs and office supplies (for the small business).

Materiality

If I purchase a fountain pen as a business item that I expect to use over a number of years, is this outlay classified as an expense or an asset? The answer lies in an accounting concept called materiality. The materiality concept means that you account for items as an asset only if the value of the item is material to the business.

The Tax Office has entered into the debate of just what is material and has put a figure of $300 on it. If you purchase an item that qualifies as an asset under the normal rules, but costs less than $300 then you can classify it as an expense. However, the total asset must cost less than $300. You cannot, for instance, break down the asset into its component parts, each of which costs less than $300 and expense the lot. Materiality is a total concept.

However, if your turnover is less than $2 million dollars then you can class yourself as a small business entity for taxation reasons and then the materiality limit is increased to $1000. This is a taxation concession to small businesses which is referred to as the simplified depreciation rules.

We therefore have two materiality limits: $300 for businesses with a turnover of more than $2 million and $1000 for small business entities with a turnover of less than $2 million.

The cost of an asset—GST or no GST?

If I purchase an item of equipment for $1100 including GST, the journal entry may be as follows:

Equipment	1000	
GST	100	
Cash at bank		1100

Therefore when we talk of the cost of an asset, we are really talking about the GST exclusive cost; that is, without the GST being included in the cost. However, if you are not registered for the GST then you cannot claim the GST offset and therefore the cost of the asset is the full GST inclusive price to you.

The cost of an asset is also the total cost including all accessories, delivery and installation expenses. In tax terms, the cost of the asset is how much it costs in situ and ready to use. For example, if you buy a lathe that required special concrete footing and a special electricity supply, then the cost of the lathe would include its purchase price, delivery, installation and the cost of the footings and electrical supply.

Second element costs

It is often the case that after you have purchased an asset you will add items to it, such as a bull bar or stereo system. Irrespective of how long after you purchased the asset and how much the add-on costs, all extras added to the asset increase its initial cost. These add-ons are called second element costs and are treated as another part of the original asset.

Repair and second element costs

If an asset needs repair, the repairs are usually classified as an expense provided that they do not add to the value of the asset but merely bring it back to its original state. For example, if I purchase a truck with a six-cylinder motor that blows in the first year and the motor is repaired with a like-for-like replacement, this is an expense.

However, if I replace the six-cylinder motor with a V8, then this is an enhancement to the original and the cost of the V8 motor is therefore a second element cost. But it is the full cost of the enhancement that is added to the asset as a second element cost, not just the difference between what the repair should have cost and what I decided to do.

Replacement items

Replacement tools are an expense irrespective of the cost, but not the initial purchase. If you purchase a set of new tools, or a tool that is not just a replacement for an existing one, then if it exceeds the $300/$1000 materiality limit you must classify this new acquisition as an asset.

The same principle applies to items such as linen in a bed and breakfast. The initial purchase of the linen for the establishment is an asset if the total cost exceeds the $300/$1000 limit. Replacement items, irrespective of the cost, are usually classified as an expense.

Accounting for assets

When you acquire an item then you must first classify that item as either an expense or an asset. If the cost of the asset is less than $300 then you can classify and treat it as an expense. For example, if you buy a $165 briefcase, it would be treated in the following way:

Office supplies	150	
GST	15	
Cash at bank		165

If the item's cost is more than $300 but less than $1000 and you are a small business entity for taxation purposes, using the simplified depreciation rules you can treat the asset as an expense. However, the expense classification is called a low cost asset and included with your other depreciation expense accounts:

Depreciation — low cost asset	900	
GST	90	
Cash at bank		990

In all other cases the item is treated and accounted for as an asset in its own right.

Depreciation and amortisation

Assets are subdivided into three classifications:

▶ *Current assets:* will provide a future benefit within the next **accounting period**, such as cash at bank or debtors. Current assets are not subject to any form of depreciation because they have a limited life.

▶ *Noncurrent assets:* also known as fixed assets, these assets are written off as an expense over their effective life.

▶ *Intangible assets:* part of noncurrent assets because they provide the business benefit over a long period. They include rights such as patents and copyrights and have a different method of depreciation, usually referred to as amortisation, which is a fixed amount over their legal life.

All noncurrent business assets, with the exception of land, are subject to some form of depreciation. However, the methodology differs greatly between small business entities using the simplified depreciation rules and other small businesses over the $2 million turnover limit.

Micro businesses using the simplified depreciation rules

We've considered how assets of $300 to $1000 are dealt with. Assets worth more than $1000 are recorded as assets in the balance sheet and are subject to depreciation.

The first stage in working out depreciation is to determine if the asset has an effective life of more than 25 years. Assets with a life in excess of 25 years have a depreciation rate of 5 per cent, while all other assets have a deprecation rate of 30 per cent. These rates are halved for the first year and halved for any second element costs (improvements or enhancements) that you add to the value of the asset in the year that these costs were added.

Let us look at a piece of equipment, purchased from MyEquip that cost $27 500 on 3 March 2011. If you purchased this item for cash, the journal entry would be:

Equipment	25 000	
GST	2 500	
Cash at bank		27 500

Along with the equipment account you would also have an account to hold the depreciation associated with this item. This account we will call equipment—accumulated depreciation. Under the standard chart of accounts, assets all start with the number 1. If we allocate the 1500–1800 series to noncurrent assets then your equipment could be:

1550	Equipment
1551	Equipment—accumulated depreciation

You will also need an expense account to hold the depreciation expense amount, which under the simplified depreciation system is called small business pool (small business long life pool for assets over 25 years). The standard chart of accounts expenses all begin with the number 6 so the depreciation expense account could be in the 6300 series:

6310	Depreciation—low cost asset
6320	Depreciation—small business pool
6330	Depreciation—small business long life pool

We need to determine the depreciation amount to be charged against this asset as at 30 June. To do this we normally create a deprecation schedule, such as the one shown in table 2.1.

Table 2.1: depreciation schedule

Date	Open value	Depreciation	Closing value
3/03/2011			25 000.00
30/06/2011	25 000.00	3750.00	21 250.00
30/06/2012	21 250.00	6375.00	14 875.00
30/06/2013	14 875.00	4462.50	10 412.50
30/06/2014	10 412.50	3123.75	7 288.75
30/06/2015	7 288.75	2186.63	5 102.13
30/06/2016	5 102.13	1530.64	3 571.49

From this schedule we can determine the value of depreciation to be charged against the asset each year. We used 15 per cent for the first year, irrespective of the date the item was purchased and 30 per cent of the closing value which we transferred to the opening value column. This is the method that is used for all assets under the simplified depreciation system with a life less than 25 years. For long-term assets we use 2.5 per cent/5 per cent rather than 15 per cent/30 per cent.

The journal entry on 30 June 2011 is:

Depreciation—small business pool   3750

     Equipment—accumulated depreciation   3750

The journal entry on 30 June 2012 is:

Depreciation—small business pool   6375

     Equipment—accumulated depreciation   6375

The expense account at the end of each year is zeroed off to the profit and loss account. We discuss this further in day 4. The accumulated depreciation keeps growing each year. The amount is not credited directly against the asset value itself, as the asset value has been accurately determined by the market, whereas the depreciation amount is only an estimate. Table 2.2 accounts for the journal entries.

Table 2.2: running balances

Equipment   1550

Date	Particulars	Folio	Debit	Credit	Balance
3/3/2011	MyEquip Ltd		25 000.00		25 000.00

Equipment—accumulated depreciation   1551

Date	Particulars	Folio	Debit	Credit	Balance
30/6/2011	Small business pool			3750.00	(3750.00)
30/6/2012	Small business pool			6375.00	(10 125.00)

Low balance assets

The above method of calculating depreciation is called the reducing balance method. The main problem with this method is that you never completely write off the asset's value. You are always left with a 'tail'.

Once the closing value (also referred to as the written down value or the adjustable value) reaches a point where it is no longer viable to continue to treat the asset as a separate entity, then you should transfer the balances of the asset and its accumulated depreciation account into the one account called small business pool. This account is an asset account and should not be confused with the similar sounding expense account depreciation—small business pool.

Disposal of an asset

How do we account for the disposal by sale, scrap or trade-in of one of our assets?

At this point we diverge from the IFRS standard, but as we are dealing with a small business with a turnover of less than $2 million, we are not required to abide by the IFRS standards as published by the AASB. Instead we will use the Tax Office method.

When you dispose of an asset it will have a value, be it the value as an item sold or traded-in or just scrap value. If you simply give it away then it will still have a market value. It is this value that we need to account for.

Step 1. At the time of the disposal post the credit side of the disposal journal to an asset account called the small business pool.

Step 2. If you have not already done so, transfer the original historical asset cost and its accumulated depreciation balance into the small business pool account.

After transferring the asset's original cost, accumulated depreciation amount and the value of the disposal into the small business pool account you usually end up with a debit balance in the account. This occurs if you made a loss on the disposal or there were already sufficient debit balances in the pool from other assets to absorb any profit you may have made on disposal. Any debit balance in the pool is then depreciated by 30 per cent in the normal manner, but the depreciation amount is credited directly against the pool balance and not against a separate accumulated depreciation account.

However, if the disposal was for a profit and the pool balance is in credit, you still continue to depreciate the pool balance in the normal manner, with the exception that now the depreciation is a debit adjustment against the other credit depreciation amounts.

As an example, let us assume that we have plant to be depreciated by $1000, equipment to be depreciated by $600 and a pool balance in credit for $300. The amount of depreciation we charge against the pool is 30 per cent or $90. The journal entry is:

Accumulated depreciation plant	1000	
Equipment — accumulated depreciation	600	
Small business pool		90
Depreciation — small business pool		1510

The total of all closing values is in credit

The total closing value of all your assets, including the small business pool, must always be debit. If you dispose of an asset at a profit so that the credit balance in the pool overrides the debit balance of all other assets, then you must transfer all of your assets and their associated accumulated depreciation accounts into the small business pool. The outstanding credit balance of the small business pool is then transferred to the other income — profits on disposal of an asset account.

The total of all closing values is less than $1000

If the total of all of the closing values of all of your assets, including the small business pool balance, is less than $1000 you can transfer all of your assets and their associated accumulated depreciation accounts into the small business pool. The outstanding debit balance can then be deducted in full by transferring it to the depreciation—small business pool account. Effectively all of your assets now have a zero balance.

GST included in the cost

When you dispose of an asset for which you have previously claimed a GST credit, then you must include an amount of GST in the disposal. Technically such an amount is a GST adjustment, but because the credit to which it applies is outside the current BAS period, you treat the GST as you would any other taxable sale (taxable supply). The values used above are all exclusive of the GST component.

Standard depreciation rules (capital allowances)

If your business's turnover exceeds $2 million or for other reasons you cannot use the simplified depreciation rules, then the capital allowances rules apply. Again, because we are discussing a small business with a turnover of less than $20 million, the IFRS rules do not apply. Instead we are governed by the tax rules. Fortunately, in practice there is little difference between IFRS and capital allowances (depreciation).

Assets to which the capital allowance rules do not apply

Land is not subject to a depreciation charge under accounting or tax rules. Neither are assets that you have not allocated to the business but charge the business for their use, such as cars under the cents per kilometre method (see day 7).

Capital works such as buildings are handled differently under accounting and tax rules. We discuss how to handle them in the section 'Special rules' on p. 45.

Low cost assets of less than $1000

When you purchase an item whose cost exceeds $300 that is to be accounted for under the normal capital allowance rules you are required to record that acquisition as an asset. However, if the cost is less than $1000 (for the whole asset, not just its constituent parts) then you can allocate the purchase to a low value pool and depreciate the pool balance by 37.5 per cent each year (18.75 per cent for the first year). The depreciated amount is credited directly against the pool balance and not to a separate accumulated depreciation account. The depreciation expense is allocated to the depreciation—low value pool account. However, once you make the decision to allocate a low cost asset to the pool, all future low cost asset purchases must also be allocated to the pool. It's a case of one in, all in!

If you dispose of a pooled item, then you allocate the net amount received directly to the pool, reducing the pool balance. If the balance goes into credit as a result of the disposal, the credit balance becomes income to the business and is transferred to another income account, profit on disposal of an asset.

Closing value less than $1000

If your asset value, less its accumulated depreciation amount, is less than $1000 then you can allocate this closing value (accounting term) or adjustable value (tax term) to the low value pool. Unlike low cost assets, you can make this decision on an asset-by-asset basis. Your first year deduction in this instance is the full 37.5 per cent.

Assets in excess of $1000

When you purchase an asset costing more than $1000 then you must create an account to hold the asset's cost and an account to hold the asset's accumulated depreciation. If you purchase equipment then you might create the following accounts:

1670   Equipment at cost

1675   Equipment—accumulated depreciation

You should also create a depreciation expense account if you do not already have one. The depreciation account will hold the depreciation amounts for all depreciable assets as one amount. The depreciation amounts are divided across the various accumulated depreciation accounts but totalled to the depreciation expense account.

The question we must now ask is, how do we calculate the depreciation amount?

Effective life

To determine the amount of depreciation that you can claim against an asset, you must work out the effective life of the asset, then calculate the percentage of depreciation to be charged based upon that estimate. Fortunately the Tax Office produces a schedule of effective lives for most assets and if you use the commissioner's schedule you are protected in an audit from having to prove your calculations. This schedule is reproduced on my website as an Excel spreadsheet.

Learn by example

Let's assume that we purchased a concrete transit mixer on 2 November 2010 for $99 000 from My Motors. The journal entry for this purchase would look like this:

1550	Concrete transit mixer at cost	90 000	
	GST	9 000	
	My Motors sundry creditor		99 000

We now need to determine the depreciation to be charged against this asset as at 30 June 2011. However, we must first determine if we are going use the straight line method or the diminishing value method. The straight line method uses a fixed percentage of the cost each year, whereas the diminishing value applies to the written down value; that is, the cost less its accumulated depreciation. However, on the plus side the diminishing value method uses a rate 1.5 times the base straight line rate. Therefore it is normal to use the diminishing value rate and that is what we will assume from this point onwards.

Next, from the schedule on my website you will see that concrete transit mixers have an effective life of 6.67 years.

Step 1. The base percentage is worked out by the formula 1/ effective life.

$$1/6.67 = 15\%$$

Step 2. The diminishing value rate is 150 per cent of the base percentage.

$$15\% \times 1.5 = 22.5\%$$

Step 3. You can only apply this amount to the days held; that is, the number of days between the purchase date of 2 November and 30 June. That works out at 240 days.

Step 4. The depreciation that we can charge is the cost, less any accumulated depreciation to date, times the percentage, times the days held over 365.

$$\$90\,000 - 0 \times 22.5\% \times 240/365 = \$13\,315$$

If the method above is a little daunting then you can use the depreciation schedule under capital allowances that is available from my website. By plugging in the cost, date of purchase and the effective life, the schedule shown in table 2.3 is produced.

Table 2.3: depreciation schedule under capital allowances

Small business under capital allowances				
Asset		Concrete transit mixers		
Cost		$90 000.00		
Effective life		6.67 years		
Depreciation rate		22.49%		
Date	Opening value	Second element cost	Depreciation	Closing value
2/11/2010				90 000.00
30/06/2011	90 000.00		13 308.41	76 691.59
30/06/2012	76 691.59		17 246.98	59 444.60
30/06/2013	59 444.60		13 368.35	46 076.25
30/06/2014	46 076.25		10 361.98	35 714.28
30/06/2015	35 714.28		8 031.70	27 682.58
30/06/2016	27 682.58		6 225.47	21 457.11
30/06/2017	21 457.11		4 825.44	16 631.67
30/06/2018	16 631.67		3 740.26	12 891.42
30/06/2019	12 891.42		2 899.12	9 992.30
30/06/2020	9 992.30		2 247.14	7 745.15
30/06/2021	7 745.15		1 741.79	6 003.37

The first thing you should notice is the slight variation in the depreciation to be charged from $13315 to $13308.41. This is because of the more accurate calculations available under Excel. You will also notice that the depreciation schedule has provision for the addition of second element costs and is valid to 2021.

Recording the depreciation charge

The journal entry as at 30 June 2011 would look like this:

Depreciation expense	13308.41	
Concrete transit mixer — accumulated depreciation		13308.41

The journal entry as at 30 June 2012 would look like this:

Depreciation expense	17246.98	
Concrete transit mixer — accumulated depreciation		17246.98

The depreciation expense account is zeroed off each year to the profit and loss account. The accumulated depreciation account keeps accumulating the depreciation associated with the asset, as shown in table 2.4.

Table 2.4: accumulated depreciation

Concrete transit mixer — accumulated depreciation   1551

Date	Particulars	Folio	Debit	Credit	Balance
30/6/2011	Depreciation	GJ_N		13308.41	(13308.41)
30/6/2012	Depreciation	GJ_N		17246.98	(30555.39)

You should make a fresh copy of a depreciation schedule for each asset you purchase. These copies are held in an assets register (refer to the section 'Assets register' later in the chapter).

Disposal of an asset under the UCA rules

When you dispose of an asset you receive value for the sale. This could be in the form of cash, a promise to pay or as a trade-in value. We must compare this termination value (a tax term) to the closing value (cost less accumulated depreciation) of the asset to determine if you have made a profit or loss on disposal. However, we must first determine if there is any depreciation that we can charge for the use of the asset until its time of disposal.

As an example, let us assume we disposed of the concrete transit mixer on 15 December 2013 for $49 000. Did we make a profit or loss on the disposal?

First we must work out the depreciation amount for the time we still had use of the asset, then compare the final closing value with the disposal proceeds, as shown in table 2.5. Again you can use the depreciation schedule available from my website.

Table 2.5: determining profit or loss on disposal of an asset

Asset	Concrete transit mixers
Cost	$90 000.00
Effective life	6.67
Depreciation rate	22.49%
Date of last financial year	30/06/2013
Closing balance	46 076.25
Date of disposal	15/12/2013
Disposal (termination) value	49 000.00
Depreciation adjustment	4 769.35
Profit (loss) on disposal	$7 693.10

Unfortunately, accounting for the disposal is a little more complex. Firstly, we must create a clearing account called 'Disposal of asset — concrete transit mixer' and transfer the final balances into that account. The profit or loss is then transferred to the appropriate profit on sale of asset or loss on sale of asset accounts:

Depreciation expense	4769.35	
Concrete transit mixer — accumulated depreciation		4769.35
Being: the depreciation charge for the use up to time of disposal		
Disposal of asset — concrete transit mixer	90 000	
Concrete transit mixer		90 000
Being: the transfer of the cost to the disposal account		
Concrete transit mixer — accumulated depreciation	48 693.10	
Disposal of asset — concrete transit mixer		48 693.10
Being: transfer of accumulated depreciation to disposal account		
Disposal of asset — concrete transit mixer	7693.10	
Profit on sale of asset		7693.10
Being: transfer of profit on disposal to profit on sale of assets account		

Table 2.6 shows the ledger accounts that reflect the journal entries.

Table 2.6: ledger accounts

Concrete transit mixer — accumulated depreciation   **1551**

Date	Particulars	Folio	Debit	Credit	Balance
30/6/2011	Depreciation	GJ_N		13 308.41	(13 308.41)
30/6/2012	Depreciation	GJ_N		17 246.98	(30 555.39)
30/6/2013	Depreciation	GJ_N		13 368.35	(43 923.74)
15/12/2013	Depreciation	GJ_N		4 769.35	(48 693.09)
15/12/2013	To disposal	GJ_N	48 693.09		0

Disposal of asset — concrete transit mixer   **9910**

Date	Particulars	Folio	Debit	Credit	Balance
15/12/2013	Proceeds	GJ_N		49 000.00	(49 000.00)
15/12/2013	Cost	GJ_N	90 000.00		41 000.00
15/12/2013	Depreciation	GJ_N		48 693.10	(7 693.10)
15/12/2013	Profit on sale	GJ_N	7 693.10		0.00

Profit on sale of assets   **9010**

Date	Particulars	Folio	Debit	Credit	Balance
15/12/2013	Concrete mixer	GJ_N		7 693.10	(7 693.10)

Private use of business assets

One of the main areas of concern in accounting for transactions in a small business is the interaction of private and business dealings. All business owners will pay for some private expenses out of business funds, take stock for their own private use or use some of the business assets for their own private purposes. Each of these situations is handled slightly differently from both a tax and an accounting perspective. In this topic we discuss the purchase, use and disposal of business assets that have a private use component.

For example, assume that you operate a small business from your home office and that you decide to purchase a computer out of business funds for that home office. You estimate that you will use the computer about 50–50 for business and private matters.

The first thing you need to concern yourself with is GST. You can only claim a GST credit (assuming that you are registered for GST) on the business portion of the purchase.

Secondly, what you are actually doing is applying part of the capital contribution you made to the business to a private purpose. Therefore the private portion of your capital purchase needs to be an allocation of capital. I prefer to do this by means of a separate private use of assets account that is in effect a negative capital account. *Note:* the drawings account that would normally be used for private expenditure should only be used for revenue items; that is, drawings of wages, payment of private expenses out of business funds or the private use of **trading stock**.

Therefore the equity accounts could look something like the following:

3100	Capital J Smith
3150	Private use of assets J Smith
3500	Drawings J Smith
3900	Retained earnings

You purchase the computer for $3300.00 on the basis that 50 per cent of the time it will be used for private purposes:

Office equipment	1500	
GST	150	
Private use of assets	1650	
Cash at bank		3300

Notice that only 50 per cent business use has been allocated to the office equipment account and only the 50 per cent business use GST allocated to the GST account. The 50 per cent private use amount has been allocated to the private use equity account.

The above accounting can be used for all entity types and overcomes the problem of fringe benefits tax (FBT). The only concern is that in the case of a registered company, you cannot treat the private use as a loan from the company.

The private use amount is reported as a reduction in your capital contribution. In the case of partnerships or companies it can also be handled through the distribution of profits. Accounting for the private use of the purchase as above will allow your accountant to see immediately the situation and treat it correctly, according to your entity type, in the accounts at year's end.

However, the purchase of the asset is only part of the problem. When you depreciate the asset, either through a pool or as an asset in its own right, you can depreciate only the business portion of the purchase. In the case of the computer the opening value is $1500, not $3000, and the depreciation schedule will be based on this reduced amount.

A number of dollar-based limits could apply to the asset, such as the $300 initial purchase price, $1000 initial purchase price or $1000 closing value. Unlike the depreciation calculations, the dollar limit amounts are based on the full value of the asset and not just its business portion. As an example, you may be a small business entity micro business, so purchases of less than $1000 can be written off as an immediate expense. If you purchase equipment valued at $1650 then it will not fall under the $1000 limit even if 50 per cent of it is for private use and therefore you allocate only $750 to the pool.

When you sell an asset you must undertake the procedures outlined earlier, but only for the business portion of the sale proceeds. The private portion of the sale proceeds is allocated to the private use account, reducing its value. The negative side is that capital gains tax may apply to the disposal of the private use portion of a business asset.

For example, if you sell the computer for $2200 you must account for the GST on disposal because it was subject to a GST credit on acquisition:

Cash at bank	2200	
Disposal of asset (or pool)		1000
GST		100
Private use of assets		1100

Assets register

Could you easily find out the purchase date and details of your family car, as well as when the registration and insurance are due, and when was it last serviced? Now consider all the assets held by a business and all of the details we have discussed in this topic and you will see the need for a formal method of recording this information in a set of records called the assets register.

When you first purchase any asset you must open an assets file. The original purchase contract, registration, insurance and service accounts are filed in this folder. Copies of these documents become part of your accounting system as evidence of debt and to record the payment. (It is acceptable to make PDF copies of these documents and file them electronically, provided that you regularly back up your files.) The copy in your expenses file is archived and destroyed after five years. You keep your asset file until you dispose of the asset, when the file is archived and destroyed five years later. Keeping your asset file is important so that you can prove matters such as ownership and service history.

When creating your asset folder you will need to create a cover sheet divided into sections:

▶ details of the purchase

▶ details of enhancements or improvements (second element costs)

▶ service history (if required)

▶ accounting assumptions, such as private use and effective life

▶ depreciation schedule

▶ location (may not be required for small businesses).

The cover sheet is different for each class of asset; for example, the details required for a motor vehicle are substantially different from those for office furniture. Most computerised asset management systems provide a different 'mask' for each type of asset.

You may also wish to group your assets. In your accounts you may have just one account for motor vehicles and one accumulated depreciation account. You will need a separate schedule that covers all the motor vehicles in that group and details of each individual vehicle. This is often done using an Excel spreadsheet. Most computerised asset management systems provide 'group' information for your accounts.

Pooled assets are a special form of a group of assets. You will need to keep an Excel spreadsheet that details all of the entries into the pool, including the initial depreciation amount (15 per cent or 18.5 per cent as or if required).

One of the major exercises that must be done at least annually is to sight each asset and make sure that it is still performing satisfactorily. In accounting terms this is called an impairment review. The location in your cover sheet is the prime source of information for this exercise. Computerised systems are usually able to track an asset's location and print an asset count sheet or even use a barcode reader. However, a simple count sheet is sufficient for most small businesses and issuing formal transfer slips when assets change location is not usually necessary.

Special rules

The Tax Office has created many special rules limiting the amount of tax deduction that it will allow for certain capital expenditures. The Tax Law Improvement Project reduced the number of rules, but there are still quite a few traps for the unwary. In this section, a few of the more important cases are discussed.

Industrial buildings and structural improvements

Special tax rules apply to buildings that are mainly used for industrial purposes, such as factory units and motel units, which can be depreciated at a rate of 4 per cent. Sealed roads, driveways, car parks and retaining walls are considered to be structural improvements and are depreciable at 2.5 per cent. Only the owner of the structure can claim the deduction and only on the basis of the original construction cost, not any subsequent purchase price. There is no balancing adjustment on sale, but any subsequent capital gain or loss from disposal of the building is adjusted for any amounts claimed as a deduction. This reduction of the cost base applies only to property purchased after May 1997.

Primary producers

To be a primary producer you must enter into the business in a methodical manner with an expectation of profit. You must be able to prove this expectation, preferably by a business plan and projected budget. If you fail this test, but still feel that you are in business you should seek professional assistance in order to examine available alternatives.

Primary production takes many forms and includes vineyards, orchards and raising animals. Special provisions apply to primary producers. The booklet *Information for Primary Producers* is available from your local Tax Office for full details.

Software and website development costs

Software is treated like any other assets. If it cost less than $1000 it is written off to the low cost assets and if it was more than $1000 it is depreciated over a four-year effective life (25 per cent straight line). Websites are not software if they only display information, in which case they can be expensed immediately. However, if the website is interactive, such as gathering customer details and online orders, then it should be classified as a software asset and depreciated accordingly.

Software purchased before May 2008 could be written off over a 2.5 year effective life; that is, a straight line rate of 40 per cent.

Other special provisions

Some items of expenditure are classified as assets under the tax rules, but may or may not be an asset under accounting.

The costs you incur in establishing your business or to change from one structure to another must be classified as an intangible asset and amortised at 20 per cent of the cost per annum. You can deduct the full 20 per cent in the year you incur the cost, irrespective of the date you **incurred** the expenditure.

Borrowing costs of more than $100 are likewise an asset that is amortised over five years (20 per cent straight line), but in this case the first year is proportioned from the date you incurred the expenditure.

Motor vehicles—a special case

Most businesses in Australia use a motor vehicle of some kind. This is also the area that is the most grey in terms of what is private use and what is business use. Even the question of who owns the vehicle—the business or the business owner—is often not clear cut. For these reasons this is a fairly complex area to deal with.

What is a car?

A car is a passenger vehicle (except a motor cycle), including four-wheel drives, vans and other vehicles designed to carry no more than nine people and a load of less than one tonne. A luxury car limit applies to such vehicles that limits the depreciation available and can trigger the luxury car tax. The luxury car limit for 2011 is $57 466.

If the initial purchase price of a car exceeds the luxury car value for the year, then any depreciation allowable on that vehicle is limited to the luxury car limit. The GST credit in this case is limited also to one-eleventh of the car limit.

Motor vehicles owned by the business and used exclusively for business purposes are treated, with the exception of the luxury car limit, just like any other business asset. However, it is far more likely that the car will have both a business and a private use component and it is this dual use that is the cause of the problem.

A car used by the business can be 'owned' by the business irrespective of the registration details. If the car was purchased from business funds then it is an asset of the business. However, if the asset is subject to private use then you could trigger a fringe benefit problem. A detailed discussion of FBT is beyond the scope of this text; however, if the car is owned by the owners and the owner charges the business for its business use, then there are no FBT issues.

Business vehicles that are not cars

If you or your business own a delivery vehicle that is used exclusively for business purposes, or any other vehicle that *does not* satisfy the car definition, then it is handled just like any other asset. You include it with your other assets, claim the GST credit on purchase and depreciate the net amount. When you sell it, say by trade-in, it is a taxable supply and the sale is subject to GST. You write off the asset in the normal manner without any further problems. Home garaging of delivery vehicles used for deliveries between work and home will not necessarily be considered private use.

Motor vehicles that are cars require substantiation

If you own the vehicle and are going to charge the business for its use then the first step is to determine which method you are going to use to calculate the deduction.

These methods relate to the substantiation of claim in relation to motor vehicles designed to carry less than nine passengers or one tonne in weight, including four-wheel drives, panel vans and utilities, although some special rules to do with incidental use apply to panel vans in some circumstances. The substantiation rules do not apply to motor cycles, taxis or vehicles over nine passengers (buses) or one tonne (trucks) carrying capacity. The normal rules that apply to any other asset apply in these instances, including the private use provisions.

Where you own the car, there are four ways to claim the business use proportion:

▶ *Cents per kilometre.* This is limited to 5000 business kilometres per year. Anything above this limit cannot be claimed under this method and may be lost. You estimate your business kilometres for the period and multiply that by the approved rate per kilometre. The rates are available each year in the tax pack published by the Tax Office. For example, a typical two-litre sedan is 60 cents per kilometre. The estimate must be reasonable and you should be able to prove your estimate by some form of calculation, such as 'once a day to the bank for 52 weeks × 5 days (−11 public holidays) at 10k per round trip = 2490k @ 60c per k = $1494.00'.

▶ *One-third of actual expenses.* If you can prove (by estimate or log book) that your business mileage exceeds 5000 kilometres per year, then you can claim one-third of the actual expenses (including depreciation) for the year. You do not require any further proof of usage but you need to be able to prove the expenses.

▶ *Twelve per cent of original value.* If you exceed 5000 kilometres of business use per year, you can claim 12 per cent of the original value. No further substantiation, apart from proof of the original value, is required.

▶ *Log book method.* This is the only method by which you can claim your actual expenses. You must keep a log book for at least 12 weeks in the first year to establish your business use as a percentage of total kilometres travelled during the period. You then apply that percentage to the actual expenses for the period, including your depreciation expense.

These methods may sound difficult, but are easily achieved provided that the calculations are done on a regular basis. I strongly suggest that your calculations be done on a quarterly basis.

GST and substantiation

You can only claim the GST credit for the expense that you actually incur and for which you have a tax invoice that shows the GST amount. If the purchase is for an amount less than $50, such as petrol, then just a receipt will do.

The amount that you can claim depends upon the method of substantiation you use. Add up all of the GST amounts for the period, then you can claim a percentage of that total as a GST credit in the GST paid account.

If you use the *cents per kilometre* method then you can claim the percentage of your total GST credits shown in table 2.7.

Table 2.7: determining claimable GST

Estimated kilometres travelled for a creditable purpose for a year	Assumed extent of creditable purpose
0–1250	5%
1251–2500	10%
2501–3750	15%
3751–5000	20%
5000+	33.33%

If you use the *one-third of actual expenses* or the *12 per cent of original value* methods then you can claim 33.33 per cent of your total GST credits.

If you use the *log book* method to determine your business kilometres, you can use the same percentage that you use for income tax to calculate the percentage of total GST credits that you can claim.

Claiming the GST on motor vehicle purchases

If you purchase a private vehicle that you are going to use for business purposes, then you can also claim the estimated business proportion of the GST paid on the car in your business records. However, if your actual business use differs from your estimate you may be required to adjust the GST credits to reflect the new business use percentage. The best advice is to be conservative when estimating your business use on the purchase of a new vehicle.

The Tax Office position is that you can claim an **input tax credit** where the entity (your business):

▶ acquired the motor vehicle solely for use in the enterprise it is carrying on

▶ registered the motor vehicle under the name of another individual, for example the business owner

▶ provided the money or credit for the purchase of the motor vehicle and the other individual, the business owner, did not. That is, you did not use your 'private funds' to purchase the vehicle.

▶ holds a valid tax invoice for the acquisition of the motor vehicle that lists the entity as the purchaser.

Disposal of the motor vehicle

When it comes to selling the motor vehicle, the treatment varies according to who has claimed ownership of the vehicle and the method used to account for private use. There is also the added complexity of GST for taxpayers registered for GST purposes.

Balancing charge event

The term *balancing charge* refers to the final depreciation calculation that is made when you dispose of any asset. If you leased the vehicle and did not claim any depreciation for the vehicle, but did claim the lease payments in full, then no balancing charge event is applicable. It only applies to the depreciation amount claimed.

If you own the vehicle and pay all expenses from your private funds and then claim for business use on the business, the disposal of the motor vehicle is a private matter. You claim on the business for the business use up to the time of disposal and then any balancing charge is include in your own tax return.

If you use the substantiation method to claim your business use and you have only ever used the cents per kilometre or the 12 per cent of original cost methods, then no balancing charge is required on disposal.

If you used the one-third of expenses method or the log book method to determine the percentage of expense claimed, or a mixture of all four methods, then claimed this against your personal income tax, a balancing charge must be worked out.

If you are a **sole trader** and have been paying all of the expenses from your business funds and adjusting those claims according to the substantiation rules—that is, you were just claiming the business proportion as if you were a private individual claiming motor vehicle expenses according to substantiation—then the balancing charge is included in your tax return as part of your business expenses or income (it can be positive).

Cars for employees

Employers have four options when providing cars for business use by employees. These are as follows:

▶ Allow the employee to claim business use of their own private vehicle against the company when it is used for business purposes. This method is not recommended, apart from incidental once off use, as it raises problems with GST and has possible FBT implications.

▶ Give the employee an allowance as part of their **salary** package, possibly including a petrol allowance as well. The allowance is part of the salary package of the employee and is again included as income to the employee, with the employee able to claim business use on their own tax return via the substantiation method.

▶ You can provide a car that is to be used strictly for business purposes. No private use is permitted. With the exception of delivery type vehicles, no travel to or from work or overnight home garaging is permitted. Usually such an arrangement is not applicable to small businesses and is usually the province of large corporations running pool cars (business cars made available to employees as required). The only exception is for vans and other types of delivery vehicles whose use should be kept under very tight control to ensure no unauthorised private use occurs.

▶ The business pays for a motor vehicle that is then 'given' to the employee to be used for business purposes. Fringe benefits tax is payable by the employer on the private use of such a vehicle.

Revision exercise for day 2

Assume that you are a small business with a turnover of more than $2 million and that the following asset is used 60 per cent of the time in the business. You are registered for the GST and all costs are GST inclusive.

On 16 March 2011 you purchase a wood-working lathe for $4950.

On 1 November 2014 you sell the lathe for $3630.

Provide the **general journal** entries for the purchase, annual depreciation and sale of the asset.

Day 3

Inventory

Key terms and concepts

▶ *Inventory:* US term for goods you purchase for resale at a profit.

▶ *Trading stock:* alternative British term for inventory.

▶ *Cost:* all amounts expended on the purchase of an inventory item until the time the goods reach your warehouse.

▶ *Cost of sales (often referred to as cost of goods sold or COGS):* the cost of inventory, adjusted for opening and closing values.

▶ *Closing value:* the cost of inventory as established by a stocktake on the last day of the financial year, usually 30 June.

▶ *Opening value:* the closing value on the last day of the financial year is rolled over to the opening value of the new year, usually 1 July. The opening value *must* be equal to the previous closing value.

▶ *Natural increase:* in relation to livestock means stock born on the property rather than stock purchased.

▶ *Net realisable value:* the net amount that an entity expects to realise from the sale of inventory in the ordinary course of business.

▶ *Fair value (or market value):* the amount for which the same inventory could be exchanged between knowledgeable and willing buyers and sellers in the marketplace.

▶ *Periodic:* a system of inventory control and valuation where the carrying values are established by periodic stocktake.

▶ *Perpetual:* a system of inventory control where the carrying value of inventory is continuously updated.

What is inventory?

Inventory is the goods purchased for resale in the normal course of business. For a shoe store, inventory is the shoes and accessories that stock the shelves. In the case of a plumber, inventory is the fittings and other items used on the job. Inventory of a mine is the stockpile of ore mined from the ground.

Inventory also includes items you purchase that are going to be turned into goods for sale; that is, raw materials and partly completed stock items. Examples include the timber stocks of a cabinet-maker as well as the cabinet fittings and partly constructed furniture, which are referred to as work in progress.

Not all entities have inventory. Service industries such as lawyers or accountants sell a service rather than goods and therefore would not normally carry inventory items. Some service industries use a combination of goods and services, such as plumbers or electricians, who sell an installation service as well as goods used in the provision of that service, such as pipes and fittings.

It is not always easy to define what is inventory. If you consider the earlier example of a mine, ore is regarded as inventory when it is severed from the ground, but when does that occur? Is it when the ore is blasted, when it is put into a truck or when it reaches the stockpile? A further complication is that extracted ore is of varying grades, from overburden which contains no useable ore, to 100 per cent pure and all grades in between. At what grade does the extracted dirt change from a cost of extraction to an inventory item for resale? Fortunately most of us will never have to ponder such questions, but bringing it down to a small business level, is a plumber's stock of welding rods or the cabinet-maker's pots of glue inventory or consumables?

Asset, inventory or consumable?

Whenever we purchase an item we must identify and classify it within the terms of our accounting system. Often the classification is obvious, but sometimes it isn't. For example, if I purchase a motor vehicle you would probably assume that I am purchasing an asset, but what if my business is a used car yard? The purchase of a car for the manager's sole use would normally be an asset of the business, whereas the purchase of a car for the car lot would be inventory.

Let's revisit our plumber.

▶ If the plumber buys a fitting for use in a client's job, either as part of the van's general stock or as a direct purchase for a specific job, such a fitting is an inventory item.

▶ If the plumber buys general use items such as pipes, joins and general fittings, these are also inventory items even if they are van stock to be used as required. As these items are used they should be allocated to the job; for example, 30 metres of pipe, three elbows and six joins.

▶ If the plumber buys items that will be consumed on the job but will not form part of the final product, such as gas, welding rods, lubricant and rags, these are consumables that should be expensed at the time of purchase rather than allocated as an inventory item. This may not be the case for a plumbing supply company or a plumber's warehouse, but for an average plumber this is the correct treatment.

▶ If the plumber buys equipment or tools, then they are purchasing an asset (the treatment of assets is discussed in day 2).

Cost of inventory

When you purchase an item of inventory, often the cost is just the amount you pay for it. Sometimes, however, the cost also includes additional expenditure such as freight inwards, customs duties and clearance charges.

The cost of inventory includes all costs incurred to bring the item to a place where it is usable by you. This could be into your store, in your van or to your client's premises. Once in location, all other costs are expenses in their own right.

For example, if you import goods, the cost of those goods includes all costs until the goods are delivered into your control, which may include overseas freight, clearance costs, customs and GST paid. If you purchase a switch from your local hardware store, the cost of the inventory item is the amount shown on the till receipt, but if you buy an item to be delivered to a client's premises, the cost of the item includes that delivery charge.

Of course the cost of inventory includes GST. If you are registered for the GST, the cost is divided between inventory and the GST credit. If you are not registered the cost is the full amount paid.

Unlike an asset, there is no minimum amount when you purchase an inventory item. Every item of inventory purchased is recorded irrespective of its value.

Recording inventory purchases

Two systems are in place for recording the purchase and sale of an inventory item—the periodic and the perpetual inventory systems. There are therefore two systems for accounting for inventory and this includes two different systems of determining the profit on sale of these items. Neither system is better than the other; both will produce identical results.

It is important to distinguish between the accounting methodology and the inventory recording system itself. The periodic method records only limited information in the accounting system while the perpetual method records inventory purchases in detail. However, using the bare bones (periodic) approach for your accounting system does not prevent you from keeping a separate and detailed inventory recording system. This was the norm until computerised accounting systems became widespread.

Periodic inventory system

The periodic inventory system is used to record the purchase and sale of inventory under manual bookkeeping methodology. Tracking of inventory items is usually done separately on a card register system, one card for each separate inventory item. The cards under this system usually only track the amount of goods on hand, not their cost (see table 3.1, overleaf).

Table 3.1: the periodic inventory system

Widgets — 14cm gold-plated with X-over coupling

Date	Detail	In	Out	Balance
1/10/11	Order 457	120		120
3/10/11	Invoice 992		20	100
4/10/11	Invoice 994		60	40
9/10/11	Order 461	120		160

When accounting for purchases under this system, all amounts are debited to a cost of sales account called purchases. There is no attempt to distinguish one item from another; they are all grouped together as one expense item, as shown in table 3.2.

Table 3.2: accounting for purchases

Purchases account   5100

Date	Description	Folio	Dr	CR	Balance
1/10/11	Order 457 widgets		1920.00		1920.00
3/10/11	Order 458 bulbs		314.67		2234.67
7/10/11	Order 459 rope		54.99		2289.66
9/10/11	Order 460 wire		16.20		2305.86
9/10/11	Order 461 widgets		1920.00		4225.86

Additional items that add to the cost of inventory are also entered into the cost of sales expense account, each under their own account such as freight inwards or insurance. When an item is sold it is simply credited to the revenue account called sales without any attempt to match the cost of the item to the sale, as shown in table 3.3.

Table 3.3: accounting for sales

Sales account   4100

Date	Description	Folio	Dr	CR	Balance
3/10/11	Invoice 992 widgets			480.00	(480.00)
3/10/11	Invoice 993 bulbs			212.90	(692.90)
4/10/11	Invoice 994 widgets			1440.00	(2132.90)
5/10/11	Invoice 995 rope			28.16	(2161.06)

At least annually, but more commonly quarterly, you must determine the profit you've made on sales. This has to be calculated each time that it is required as a separate calculation from the purchase and sales accounting itself.

The first step in determining your profit on the transactions for the period is to determine the end-of-period value of your stock on hand. This is usually determined through an end-of-period (usually end-of-year) physical stocktake. The key to this exercise is that when you sell an item, you sell it from your current stock. When you purchase an item of stock it could be still on the shelf at the end of the period. So the cost of the goods you sell can be determined from the following formula:

Cost of sales = opening stock + purchases – closing stock

The opening stock figure is the closing stock figure from the last period. This is an accounting rule—the opening value of any one period must match exactly the closing value of the previous period. This closing stock figure will be recorded in an asset account called inventory. Under the periodic system, the inventory account is only created by the result of the stocktake values and is not adjusted for any purchase or sale figure.

The profit you make on trading can be expressed as:

Trading profit = sales – cost of sales

Putting this all together into a trading account it looks like the following:

Sales		2161.06
Less cost of sales		
Opening stock	5350.66	
Plus purchases	4225.86	
Goods available for sale	9576.52	
Less closing stock	7623.90	1952.62
Trading (gross) profit		208.44

Perpetual inventory system

The perpetual inventory system was originally used only for very high cost items, such as jewellery or motor vehicles. However, since the introduction of computerised accounting, this methodology has become standard practice in accounting for all inventory items. The primary reason for this is the ability to exactly match the cost of an item with its sale price.

A manual card record under the perpetual inventory system may look like table 3.4.

Table 3.4: the perpetual inventory system

Widgets—14cm gold plated with X-over coupling

Date	Detail	In	In ($)	Out	Out ($)	Balance	Balance ($)
1/10/11	Order 457	120	16.00			120	1920.00
3/10/11	Inv 992			20	16.00	100	1600.00
4/10/11	Inv 994			60	16.00	40	640.00
9/10/11	Order 461	120	16.50			160	2620.00
9/10/11	Inv 995			40 25	16.00 16.50	95	1567.50

You will notice quite a few differences between this card record and the previous card under the periodic system, the main difference being the inclusion of dollar amounts as well as the volume.

You will also notice that the dollar amounts apply to the purchase of the inventory as well as the sale. This is particularly evident in the last record that records a sale of 65 items but on two lines: 40 at a unit cost of $16.00 and 25 at a unit cost of $16.50. These dollar values are the cost of the items sold, not the sale value which is a completely different matter.

Under the periodic system the inventory account was established by the value of the annual stocktake. Under the perpetual method, the purchase of inventory and the sale of inventory directly alter the inventory account's balance.

Purchase of inventory under the perpetual inventory system

When you purchase an inventory item under the perpetual method, the inventory record that relates to the item is not dated with the purchase details. The total value of all of the inventory records in the inventory **subsidiary ledger** is the value of the inventory account. In this case the inventory account is a **control account** and functions in a similar manner to the debtors and **creditors control** accounts.

For example, we purchase $110 of widgets as inventory. Under the periodic model the transaction may look like the following:

Purchases	100	
GST	10	
Cash		110

Under the perpetual method the same transaction may look like:

Inventory (widgets)	100	
GST	10	
Cash		110

Notice the double description on the first line—inventory (widgets). This is because it is not only debited to the widgets record, the purchase is also debited to the inventory control account. This is the same principle applied to accounts receivable and **accounts payable** when run under the subsidiary accounts model.

Sales under the perpetual inventory system

Selling items under the perpetual inventory system is also a complicated affair. Firstly the sale is recorded in exactly the same way as before. Let us assume that on 9 October 2011 we make a cash sale for 65 widgets for $22 each. The following entry records that sale:

9/10/2011	Cash at bank	1430.00	
	Sales		1300.00
	GST		130.00

Under the periodic system, that would have been an end to the matter. However, under the perpetual model we must now update the inventory records and determine the cost of goods sold (COGS). A COGS account has been established under the cost of sales category for this purpose.

The cost of the items sold can be determined under a number of methods, such as standard cost or weighted average. We will use the most common method, first in first out (FIFO). Under this method the oldest stock is presumed to be sold first. Under this method we would have sold 40 items at $16.00 and

25 items at $16.50. To record the disposal of this inventory a further entry is required:

9/10/2011	COGS	1052.50	
	Inventory (widgets @ $16.00)		640.00
	Inventory (widgets @ $16.50)		412.50

Notice the double entry to the widgets account and the inventory account to record the difference in cost price of the items in the sale. No GST is accounted for because the inventory records are all recorded after the GST has been accounted for.

To determine the profit on sale we simply compare the sales value to the COGS:

Sales	1300.00	
Less cost of sales		
COGS		1052.50
Profit on sale		247.50

There are no opening or closing inventory values in the above calculations. This is because the cost of goods sold contains the exact cost of the goods sold, so the cost does not have to be calculated from bulk values.

The inventory account holds the value of inventory on hand at any particular time. It is not established on an annual basis but is still adjusted for obsolete and missing inventory items.

It is sometimes incorrectly stated that an annual stocktake is not required under the perpetual inventory system. The annual stocktake is not required to establish a closing value of the inventory account, but the stocktake is still required to undertake an impairment review; that is, to determine if the inventory is still accounted for and is worth its carrying value.

Computerised accounting

Computerised accounting systems are usually able to work under both inventory accounting models; however, when the system includes the accounts receivable and accounts payable modules it will invariably use the perpetual inventory method as a default. This may not be true, however, when the entity is a **service business** only. In these cases the invoices are usually created manually, even though you are using your accounting system to do this, which is akin to using your accounting system's invoice generator as a typewriter.

Inventory management systems

Most computerised accounting systems have an accounts receivable (debtors) and an accounts payable (creditors) module that is tightly linked to the inventory management system. The fact that you are running these systems does not prevent you from accounting for the GST and income tax on a cash basis; it simply depends on what point the general ledger is updated with the credit transactions, on creation or on settlement.

The creditors' system creates the **purchase orders** from the information held in the inventory system with supplier, order quantities, cost and so on. It receives the goods in and also accounts for the settlement of the debt. This is done through the accounts payable module rather than the cash payments journal as it would in a manual system.

The debtors' system creates the invoices for your customers and the delivery advice, as well as receiving the payment through the accounts receivable module rather than the cash receipts journal. Both modules continuously update the inventory management system with the goods ordered, received and dispatched, usually under the perpetual model.

In manual systems the creditors and debtors subsidiary ledgers account only for the amounts owing to your suppliers and from your customers. They do not interact with the manual inventory records which you must keep updated as a separate exercise, hence the common use of the periodic inventory model in manual systems.

One big difference between the two systems is in the handling of cash purchases of inventory and cash sales. In the manual system these are handled through the cash payments and cash receipts journals. In the computerised system you create a supplier and a customer called cash and create the **credit purchase** and sales in the normal manner, but you receipt in the payment at the same time you create the invoice through the sales and purchase modules and not separately through cash receipts and payments modules.

Small business entity (micro businesses)

If you have a turnover of less than $2 million you may use the concessions afforded to you by the Tax Office. The main concession is that you account for your purchases and sales only when you actually pay for them. This system is called the cash-based model.

Under this model you can still have credit purchases and **credit sales**; it is just that the control accounts will not be updated until the accounts are settled. This also applies to the GST component of the sale. This concept is best conveyed by the following illustration.

On 25 March we sell an item for $3300.00 to Mrs Jones on credit terms of a 10 per cent discount if paid within 10 days and net 30 days. Under normal accounting rules, we firstly record the sale:

25/3/2011	Accounts receivable (Mrs Jones)	3300.00	
	Sales		3000.00
	GST		300.00

The sale is recorded as income in April and the GST included in the third quarter BAS. Mrs Jones settles her account on 2 April and claims the 10 per cent discount.

2/4/2011	Cash at bank	3000.00	
	Discount allowed	272.73	
	GST adjustment	27.27	
	Accounts receivable (Mrs Jones)		3300.00

The GST adjustment is now included in the fourth quarter BAS.

On a cash basis, the sale is recorded on an accounts receivable system external to the accounting system. When it is paid the accounting system is updated with the following details:

2/4/2011	Cash at bank	3000.00	
	Sales		2727.27
	GST		272.73

The GST owing on the sale is paid in the fourth quarter BAS.

As you can see from this example, working on a cash basis has a number of advantages. Most modern computerised accounting packages accommodate cash-based accounting for credit purchases and sales.

Another advantage of the cash-based system is the case of bad debts. Whenever you deal in credit you are liable to have some bad debts. In the case of **accrual accounting** you must account for the sale when it is made and you can only claim a credit for bad debts (both from an income tax and GST perspective) when you have exhausted all avenues of recovery.

In the case of a cash-based entity, because you have never been paid for the sale you did not report the sale and therefore no bad debt adjustment is required.

Another benefit of being a small business entity is that, if you can estimate that the difference between your last annual stocktake and the current stocktake is no more than $5000, under tax law you are excused from undertaking the stocktake.

Annual stocktake

Under accounting rules, all businesses must undertake an annual stocktake. This statement would appear to be at odds with the small business tax concession discussed above, but in my opinion you would put yourself at a tax disadvantage not to undertake a full stocktake at the end of each year. Sooner or later an estimate will have to be backed up by an accurate stocktake and it is at this time that the past estimated position will be adjusted.

We discuss three separate scenarios in this section, each one depending upon the inventory records that you keep:

▶ *perpetual* — full records of quantities on hand and cost

▶ *periodic* — full records of quantities only

▶ *none* — no separate inventory register kept.

The rules in regard to annual stocktakes under IFRS, GAAP and tax are almost identical to such an extent that we do not have to differentiate. The purpose of the annual stocktake is to:

▶ verify that the item actually exists. Items do go missing.

▶ check that the item is in good condition and has not deteriorated, gone out of date or has become obsolete. In accounting terms this process is known as an impairment review.

▶ determine its cost within the limits set by the tax law, cost, market selling or replacement. This can be done on an item-by-item basis, but is usually applied across the board, with the exception of obsolete stock that is usually valued at the lower of cost, replacement or selling price.

The value you apply to your trading stock should be consistent from year to year. Pick one method and stick to it! This will minimise your tax liability variations. *A note of caution*: it is an easy path for a new accountant to reduce your current tax liability by manipulating the value of your trading stock on hand, but this is a short-sighted approach that will simply cause you problems next year.

It should also be emphasised that you can only apply the valuation options to your closing stock as part of the annual stocktake process. Your opening stock for next year will be exactly equal to your closing stock figure from this year; it will be this year's closing stock figure rolled over into next year.

Inventory valuation methods

If you are conducting a normal trading business—that is, you buy and sell goods, such as a corner deli or a plumber—then your trading stock at the end of the year is valued in the following way:

▶ *Cost.* This is what the inventory item cost you, including all costs up to the point it was ready and available for sale. Usually this means all costs up to your warehouse door and includes inwards freight and insurance, even though these items have been separately recorded as expenses in your accounting system. The cost of items under this option assumes the first in first out (FIFO) method of stock rotation has been used.

▶ *Replacement.* This is what the item would have cost, under normal conditions, if it had been purchased on the last day of the financial year. This is not a one-off sale value but its normal replacement value.

▶ *Selling value.* This is the price that you would charge your customers under normal trading conditions.

Under accounting rules, the trading stock is valued at the lower of cost or selling, but under tax law you can choose which of these to apply, including replacement as an alternative to actual cost. There are also other methods of valuation. For example, if you are in a manufacturing business you can use full absorption costing, but that discussion is beyond the scope of this text.

Methods that should not be used include retail mark-up, weighted average or standard cost (these methods can be used as a last resort if the results of such methods approximate the cost of the inventory items). These methods are available to you for internal management purposes but should not be used for external reporting. You should note that the last in first out (LIFO) method is banned under both tax and accounting standards.

If you are registered for the GST, then the value of your trading stock does not include the GST component.

Procedures for undertaking an annual stocktake

Annual stocktakes are mandatory for all businesses. However, a lot of businesses choose to conduct stocktakes more regularly, either quarterly, monthly or, in the case of tobacco and spirit warehouses, on a weekly basis. How often you conduct a stocktake is a management decision based upon how vulnerable your stock is to pilferage or spoilage.

The annual stocktake also presents an opportunity to review not only your stock holdings but also your pricing structure. The process should really be called an inventory review rather than a stocktake, because the process of counting the stock is just a part of the whole process.

At what date?

Your stocktake should be undertaken on 30 June each year. If this is not possible then you should undertake it as close to the end of the financial year as possible, then adjust the figures back to 30 June.

Step 1 — stocktake sheets

The first step is to print a stocktake sheet for your inventory records giving you a list of all of the quantities held for all of your stock items. You do not normally record dollar figures at this stage, just quantities.

In some cases you won't have any records of your stock levels. This could be the case of an electrician whose inventory is their van stock. In these cases it is good practice to establish the ideal stock levels and then use those ideals as your basis for the stocktake.

In most small businesses the stock level is small and in a discrete area, but in larger organisations the stocktake sheets should be printed by location to make the location and counting of stock items easier. Occasionally stock will be in two separate locations. These should be treated separately and only amalgamated at the end of the process.

Counting stock is not just a sighting exercise but also an exercise of review. All items should be assessed and all damaged or obsolete stock, such as food products that are out of date, should be moved to a separate location and dealt with separately. Bulk items need not be unpacked but the outer box should be inspected, as far as possible, for damage.

Step 2 — records update

The second part of the exercise is to update the inventory register with the new stock on hand figures. Any significant differences should be brought to the notice of management and a second stocktake undertaken to verify the figures.

Step 3 — records review

Stock levels should now be reviewed. Are you carrying too much stock or not enough? Is the damage or obsolescent levels too high? Is pilfering of stock a problem? Inventory is dead money. It should be kept to a working level where you have enough to satisfy current demand but not anything in excess.

This is an ideal time for businesses without a formal inventory recording system to review their stock levels and their recording methodology. This is especially the case of tradesmen's vans. How many 'dead' items lie for years in the bottom of the tray without a second thought being given?

Valuation

There is no right or wrong method when valuing inventory. The trick is to select the method that best suits you and stick with it. Consistency is the key! Accountants who try to adjust inventory figures to make the best position possible for this year only have to pay the price next year.

In theory you have three choices when valuing inventory: cost, selling or replacement.

If you are running a perpetual inventory system where the system can produce accurate cost figures then the cost option is available to you, but in most other cases the work involved in establishing the cost is prohibitive.

In most cases you can work out what it would cost you to purchase the stock items today. This is replacement costing, but again it usually involves a lot of work.

Market selling price is the price you normally sell the item for, excluding any GST component. You should have a readily available price for all of your stock items. This is one of the main requirements for any business. It is also an ideal time to review your inventory pricing and adjust your inventory values accordingly. The market selling value is what you would sell your goods for in your market. It is not a sales value or one offered for volume discounts. Most small businesses find that the market selling value is the easiest to use and, if used consistently, gives the best results.

Tax considerations

The lower the closing stock values, the higher your cost of sales deduction and therefore the lower you taxable income will be. The temptation is therefore to reduce your closing stock value to its lowest possible amount, irrespective of the amount of work involved.

The problem is that the lower the opening value, the higher will be your taxable income next year and because the opening stock value must be exactly the same as last year's closing stock value, you have conflicting needs. The answer is consistency. You can use any of the three methods consistently and they will give you consistently the same tax result. If you manipulate the value (legally) then you can manipulate your taxable position, but it is only a timing delay. What you save today you'll owe tomorrow, so be consistent.

Inventory internal control systems

Everything that one staff member does in a business should be checked by another; no one staff member should undertake any transaction from start to finish.

Inventory can be highly susceptible to theft. If the person in charge of the inventory accounting is the same person in charge of undertaking the annual stocktake, then you have an **internal control** problem. There have been many instances of warehouse staff stealing from the business inventory.

The purchase of inventory should not be part of the duties of the warehouse staff who receive the goods into store. They should be two separate duties, so that no staff member can order goods from an 'associate' and then bring the goods into store when in fact the goods don't really exist. If that person also is responsible for the stocktake and then writes those goods off as damaged in store, who would be the wiser?

Often the main culprits for the removal of stock without authority are the sales staff. All sales staff and especially the sales manager should be banned from the warehouse. If they require display stock they should be required to raise a no-charge invoice and have those items charged to the advertising account. Failure to keep the sales staff under control is a main reason for stock discrepancies.

Private use of inventory

It is normal practice for the owners of small businesses to take items from the shelf or to purchase goods through the business. For example, a business purchases a television for $3300. On receipt into the business the journal entry is:

Television	3000	
GST	300	
Cash at bank		3300

However, this television never reaches the business premises but is delivered directly to the owner's home. Therefore the records need to be adjusted by reversing this purchase:

Drawings	3300	
Television		3000
GST		300

This transaction could just as easily have been an item of trading stock. You will notice that the television was not 'sold' to the business owners but the purchase was reversed out to the owner's drawings account, being careful to fully adjust the GST.

In some cases the owner's use of the business inventory cannot be easily accounted for and to overcome that problem the Tax Office has issued a ruling on what the owners of these particular kinds of businesses would normally take from inventory in any given year. The schedule for the value of goods taken from trading stock for private use in the 2009–10 income year is shown in table 3.5.

Table 3.5: schedule for the value of goods taken from trading stock for private use in the 2009–10 income year

Type of business	$ amount (excluding GST) for adult/child over 16 years	$ amount (excluding GST) for child 4–16 years
Bakery	1130	565
Butcher	760	380
Restaurant/cafe (licensed)	3860	1540
Restaurant/cafe (unlicensed)	3080	1540
Caterer	3330	1665
Delicatessen	3080	1540
Fruiterer/greengrocer	810	405
Takeaway food shop	2920	1460
Mixed business (includes milk bar, general store and convenience store)	3680	1840

Work in progress

The amount that can be included in your trading stock as work in progress is that amount for which you can claim a payment from your client as a legally enforceable debt. Incomplete work such as a half-finished computer program or a partially complete audit is not usually considered as trading stock.

Work in progress is also included in your closing trading stock. However, only the amount of work that has not yet been billed is work in progress. For example, if you issued an account at 'plate height' then only that part of the building above plate height can be included as work in progress. The remainder up to plate height is completed.

The value of work in progress includes all costs that you have included as expenses in your accounts; that is, the value of all material and all wages, for example, but not any profit margin.

Primary production—livestock

Livestock you have raised for sale is considered to be trading stock for accounting and tax purposes. The cost you use is the item's cost, market or selling price, just like any other item of trading stock; however, natural increases (stock born on the property as opposed to purchased stock) can also be valued at special rates as published by the Tax Office. For example, cattle, horses or deer are $35 per head, pigs $12, emus $8, goats and sheep $4, and poultry 35c.

You account for your sales and purchases of livestock in the same way as you account for other items of trading stock.

Revision exercise for day 3

1   Record the following purchases of inventory into both a periodic and a perpetual inventory card.

1/9/11	16 widgets for $26.00 each
2/9/11	27 widgets for $26.00 each
3/9/11	18 widgets for $28.00 each
4/9/11	14 widgets for $28.00 each
5/9/11	22 widgets for $30.00 each
6/9/11	25 widgets for $31.00 each
7/9/11	12 widgets for $31.50 each

In addition, on 3 September 40 widgets were sold at $35.00 each and on 5 September, 50 at $38.50 each.

2   On 8 September we sold 40 widgets at $38.00 each. Record this sale in a general journal under both the periodic system and the perpetual system.

Day 4

End of year

Key terms and concepts

▶ *Accounting period:* the financial year.

▶ *Accrual:* to accrue (record) an amount as it is earned or due, rather than when it is paid or settled.

▶ *End of year:* the last day of the financial year.

▶ *End-of-year adjustments:* adjustments required to bring the income in line with the expenses for the period.

▶ *Financial year:* in Australia this is usually 1 July to 30 June, but can be modified in some circumstances.

▶ *Impaired:* damaged or obsolete; not worth the value currently recorded in your books of account.

What is end of year?

The bookkeeping cycle is based on the calendar month. You enter the relevant transactions for the month, complete the bank reconciliation to prove the bank balances and then create the trial balance report. The BAS flows from this process. And then you start all over again!

The accounting cycle is based on the concept of an accounting year. In Australia that year is from 1 July to 30 June in the next calendar year. Each one of the bookkeeping months from July to June is added together to make one annual report. We start with an annual trial balance, which is a trial balance that covers the whole accounting year and not just one discrete month. This month-by-month bookkeeping cycle and the annual review is known as the periodic convention—all of the accounts work is broken into distinct periods.

Three reports are produced from the annual trial balance:

▶ statement of financial position (usually known as the balance sheet)

▶ statement of financial performance (usually known as the income statement)

▶ statement of cash flows.

In this book we deal only with the balance sheet and income statement.

Bookkeeping, accounting and taxation

The monthly bookkeeping cycle produces the monthly or quarterly BAS that handles the firm's GST liability. The annual accounting cycle produces the income statement that determines the business profits for the period. It is these profits that are the basis for the calculation of the business's income tax liability.

The end-of-year process

The end-of-year process really begins with the annual stocktake undertaken on the last day of the financial year. However, the actual **accounting process** cannot start until the last bookkeeping month has been completed; that is, the final bank reconciliation and trial balance have been prepared. This is often well into the next financial year.

However, preparations for year end can start well before that. You should start a debtors' review up to three months before the end of year. This is discussed further in day 5. You should also ensure that your assets and inventory registers are all completely up to date at year's end. The impairment review of your assets can be undertaken at any time, also preferably before year's end.

The steps to be taken for the end of year are:

1 *Debtors:* about three months before year's end conduct a review of your debtors to see if any bad debts need to be written off. All recovery action for doubtful debtors and the write-off of bad debts must be complete prior to year's end.

2 *Creditors:* if you purchase inventory on credit, ensure that the outstanding balances in your books match your suppliers' statements. Check for recording errors.

3 *Inventory:* undertake an impairment review of inventory to ensure that obsolete or out-of-date stock is actioned appropriately; that is, its **book value** is reduced to a realistic figure or the stock written off altogether. This process can also be repeated at the time of the annual stocktake, but weeding out troublesome items before this process saves valuable time during the stocktake.

4 *Assets:* at this stage you should review the assets register and ensure that it is completely up to date. Start a depreciation schedule that allows for the depreciation adjustment to be entered on the last day of the financial year as an end-of-year adjustment, usually using period 13. You should also conduct a physical inventory verification to ensure that all registered assets still exist and are in good condition. This annual requirement is best undertaken close to year end. An impairment review is usually part of this process.

5 *Stocktake:* conduct the annual stocktake and update the inventory records as needed. This is often done in the last few weeks of the year and adjusted to reflect the closing balance as at 30 June.

6 *End-of-period bookkeeping:* undertake the final month's process, such as bank reconciliation, as quickly as possible.

7 *End-of-period adjustments:* when the bookkeeping has been completed, enter the depreciation and inventory adjustments as necessary (these are discussed later) using period 13—end-of-period adjustments if available.

8 *Accruals and prepayments:* if you are not a cash business enter the accrual and prepayment adjustments.

9 *Rollover:* this could be an automated process for computer-based systems or a series of manual journal entries.

10 *Annual reports:* you may now create the annual reports.

Impairment review of assets

Impairment review of assets is accountants' jargon for looking at all of your assets and ensuring that they are worth the amount that you are holding them at in your books. For this purpose you could classify your assets into four categories:

▶ inventory (stock on hand at end of year)

▶ physical assets such as your motor vehicle or land and any other assets subject to depreciation

▶ debtors—your accounts receivables

▶ any other assets such as trademarks or patents.

The impairment review of assets should be undertaken where possible prior to the end of the financial year, otherwise any adjustments made may not be tax effective in this year.

Inventory

You must conduct an annual stocktake of your inventory as at the last day of the year, usually 30 June. Where this is not possible then your annual stocktake figures should be adjusted back to the last day of the financial year. Although theoretically stocktake has to be done at the end of the financial year, most small businesses conduct the stocktake in the last couple of weeks and adjust the balances forward to the end of year. This gives you time to make any adjustments required for obsolete or missing stock and gives you an accurate closing inventory figure as at the end of year.

The purpose of the annual stocktake is both to verify the existence of the item of inventory and hence account for any missing items, and to put a value on the inventory itself. The impairment process conducted as part of the annual stocktake is conducted to ensure that any item no longer worth its recorded value can be adjusted down to reflect its true worth.

Examples of impairment include stock that is out of date and must be disposed of, and stock that is obsolete and no longer worth its carrying value. You should adjust your inventory records and your accounting records to ensure that the inventory asset value is a true reflection of your inventory's worth as at the end of the financial year.

Methods of inventory accounting and the inventory valuation models are discussed in day 3.

Depreciable assets

Depreciable assets are discussed in day 2. However, as part of the annual accounting process not only do you have to write off the depreciation charge against the asset, but you also need to assess the asset carrying value against its true worth. The depreciation rates that you use should be in accordance with the Tax Office effective life schedule. Because of the taxation implications of asset revaluation, you should only adjust the carrying value of a depreciable asset where there is a substantial difference between the carrying and true values.

Debtors

Invariably some customers will not be able to pay their debts. Review your debtors about three months before year's end. Closely examine all outstanding debts for any late payers and take appropriate recovery action.

Your review will lead to you classifying your customers into four categories:

▶ good—always pay on time

▶ slow—always settle their accounts but are often late

▶ doubtful—late paying and could be at risk

▶ bad—you have doubts about the recovery of the debt.

Slow customers are a management issue. They need constant supervision but do not affect your accounting position. Doubtful and bad customers may need some end-of-year accounting adjustment.

Doubtful debts

No accounting adjustment is normally made for doubtful debts in the small business sector for two reasons:

▶ doubtful debt expense that is created by the adjusting entry is not a tax deduction

▶ under IFRS (international accounting rules) any subsequent bad debt must be written off against the provision and not as an expense. This may lead to the legitimate bad debt tax deduction being over-looked.

Let us say that your debtors owe $187 900 and that 5 per cent of this debt is considered doubtful. The journal entry required would be:

Doubtful debt expense	9395.00	
Provision for doubtful debt		9395.00

Being: the creation of the provision
for doubtful debts at 5 per cent

If Mr Brown, a debtor, subsequently becomes a bad debtor owing $2200.00, the adjustment would be:

Provision for doubtful debts	2000.00	
GST adjustment	200.00	
Accounts receivable (Mr Brown)		2200.00

Being: the write off of Mr Brown's debt
against the provision

In this write off no expense account has been adjusted and therefore no tax deduction will automatically ensue.

Bad debts

Bad debts and doubtful debts are different matters. Bad debts are a deduction for income tax purposes and also give rise to a GST adjustment. However, the tax and accounting rules are fairly strict on the definition of bad debt.

You can only call a debt bad once you have exhausted all reasonable avenues for recovery. It is not good enough that the debtor is late paying or that you consider them doubtful; you must have initiated recovery action that has failed to provide you with the payment of the debt. However, you should also be aware of the concept of materiality. The proof that all reasonable steps have been taken to recover a $100 debt will be somewhat less than that required for a $1000 debt.

The journal entry for a bad debt is to write the debt off your accounts receivable records and to adjust the GST account and bad debt expense. Let us assume that a debt for Mr Jones for $2200 has gone bad. The initial entry when you sold Mr Jones the goods would look something like the following:

Accounts receivable (Mr Jones)	2200.00	
Sales revenue		2000.00
GST		200.00

The bad debt adjustment is the reverse of this:

Bad debt expense	2000.00	
GST adjustment	200.00	
Accounts receivable (Mr Jones)		2200.00

If at a later stage you receive a settlement of 10 per cent of the debt, then the entry would be:

Bank	220.00	
Bad debt settlement (other income)		200.00
GST adjustment		20.00

The GST adjustments are not necessarily being conducted in the same period as the debt was created and any subsequent recovery will likewise not necessarily be in the same period. Only bad debts written off during the year are deductible for tax purposes in that year and therefore any adjustments for bad debts must be done prior to year end.

Other assets

Assets that fall into the other assets category include all of your current assets, excluding debtors and inventory, non-depreciable noncurrent assets such as land, and intangible assets such as patents and trademarks. All of these assets need to be reviewed to ensure that their carrying value in the accounts reflect their true value.

However, because of the tax implications of such adjustments, you would only make an adjustment where there is a substantial difference in the values.

End-of-period adjustments

End-of-period adjustments is a balancing act between the requirements of accounting as stipulated in IFRS and GAAP, and tax law and procedures, in particular income tax and the GST.

GST and other taxes — end-of-period adjustments

Under GST accounting rules, the GST is accounted for when a tax invoice is raised or received, or when any payment is made, whichever occurs first. The consequence is that when you make end-of-year accounting adjustments you should ignore any GST component.

On the other hand, income tax is usually calculated using rules that approximate normal accrual accounting conventions. You will need to keep track of the adjustments made that do not approximate normal accrual accounting conventions so that your tax agent knows to back out these adjustments before calculating your income tax liability.

Categories of end-of-period adjustments

There are two categories of end-of period adjustments:

▶ adjustments required for inventory and depreciation

▶ adjustments required to match your income with the expense for the period.

Inventory

You have a number of options when valuing your inventory and your tax accountant will attempt to manipulate these to your short-term advantage. I suggest, however, that you value your inventory at either cost, if you are using the perpetual system used in MYOB, or replacement if you are using a manual or cashbook system.

Computer systems such as MYOB can track the cost of inventory items and use the perpetual system of recording discussed in day 3. If you are using MYOB in this manner you do not need any end-of-period adjustments, you merely have to adjust your inventory records for any missing or obsolete stock.

If you are using the periodic (manual) system used in manual bookkeeping or in a cash books system, you will need to enter into your records the closing value of your inventory. It would be usual to value such inventory at replacement as it is easier to get the current cost of an item than it is to scroll through your records to find the true cost.

For example, if you are an electrician and your stock is in your van, simply make a list of the items on hand, then cost them using your supplier catalogue. Under the periodic system you now have to enter the closing stock figure. However, you will already have an inventory figure in your accounts as an asset item called inventory, which we will assume is $23 568. This is the opening inventory figure from last year and must be moved into the opening inventory accounting as part of your cost of sale (CoS) calculations:

Opening inventory (CoS)	23 568.00	
Inventory (asset)		23 568.00

Let us now assume that you have conducted your annual stocktake and the resultant figure is $28 887. The journal entry required is:

Inventory (asset)	28 887.00	
Closing stock (CoS)		28 887.00

This figure is normally entered into your accounting system as soon as it has been determined.

Depreciation

Assets are discussed in day 2 and include the calculations required to determine an asset's depreciation amount. Under our end-of-period procedure you have determined the depreciation amount to be charged against each asset and have a schedule ready to be entered into your system. The schedule could resemble something like this:

Car	3000.00
Truck	4500.00
Trailer	600.00

Your published balance sheet for last year may have looked something like this:

Noncurrent assets		
Car	25 000	
Less accumulated depreciation	15 000	10 000
Truck	68 000	
Less accumulated depreciation	35 000	33 000
Trailer	12 000	
Less accumulated depreciation	10 500	1500

You now enter into the system the depreciation amounts:

Depreciation expense	8100.00	
Accumulated depreciation car		3000.00
Accumulated depreciation truck		4500.00
Accumulated depreciation trailer		600.00

After entering the above amounts you have an expense account called depreciation with an $8100 debit balance. The accumulated depreciation accounts of the various assets have increased and their carrying values decreased accordingly:

Noncurrent assets		
Car	25 000	
Less accumulated depreciation	18 000	7 000

Truck	68 000	
Less accumulated depreciation	39 500	28 500
Trailer	12 000	
Less accumulated depreciation	11 100	900

These figures should now be the same as recorded in your assets register.

End-of-year 'matching' adjustments

The accounting principle of income and expense matching requires that any income earned in a year should be reported in that year and any expense incurred in a year should also be reported in that year. In this manner any amount of income earned in any one year can be matched against the corresponding expense incurred in that year — the matching principle.

However, when the principle uses the terms 'earned' and 'incurred' it is referring to when the transaction became legally enforceable and not when the amounts were settled. This is the basis of what we have come to know as accrual accounting — accounting for income and expenses as they accrue and not when the cash changes hands.

What this means for end-of-year processing is that we must look at all of our transactions to see if any component of that transaction rightfully belongs in another period. For example, if we pay for 12 months of insurance in January to cover the January to December period, half that expenditure, which represents six months of insurance cover, belongs in the financial year ending 30 June and the other six months in the next financial year.

There is good news for those micro businesses that operate under the Tax Office cash accounting rules. Providing that all cash income or cash expense items reflect transactions that do not exceed 12 months, then no further adjustments are necessary. Micro business owners can skip the remainder of this section and carry on to producing the reports.

For accrual based businesses, four types of adjustments need to be considered so that the income earned for the period will match the expenses for the period:

► accrued income

► accrued expenses, including accrued leave payments

► prepaid income

► prepaid expenses.

Accrued income

Accrued income is money owed to you for work done and for which you could take enforcement action if the amount is not paid. In the small business environment you should examine all work outstanding as at 30 June and issue an invoice as at or prior to 30 June. However, just because you have undertaken part of a project does not mean that the work in progress (WIP) is in fact recoverable at that stage. It is often the case that no legal obligation arises until the job is finished. In these instances you will not have the right to issue an invoice, nor will you have accrued income outstanding.

Accrued income can arise in instances where you have a commission owing for work performed, but you do not expect to receive payment until a later time. Provided that the commission is business income and you are accounting for your income under an accruals regime, then the journal entry required is:

Accrued income (asset)	3000.00	
Income revenue		3000.00
Being: commissions earned for the period but not yet received		

This entry will increase your income that is subject to income tax and therefore such adjustments should be contemplated only where there is an absolute right to the payment.

When the business commission is subsequently received the journal entry is:

Bank	3300.00	
Accrued income (asset)		3000.00
GST		300.00

Being: the commission outstanding received

Your accrued income adjustments can usually be completed close to the end-of-year close-off.

Accrued expenses 1 — non-leave

You often will not start your annual report adjustments until a number of weeks after the close of year. In this time you will receive a number of invoices that relate to expenses that cover a period both before and sometimes after the end of year, such as an electricity account that covers the period 1 May to 31 July. In this case two-thirds of the account should be accounted for in the old year and only one-third of the account in the new year subsequent to 30 June.

Let us assume that the electricity account was for $3300 (including GST), of which $2200 relates to the year ended 30 June and $1100 relates to the year started 1 July. The journal entry to account for the GST exclusive electricity amount recorded in the previous year is:

30 June	Electricity expense	2000.00	
	Accrued expenses (liability)		2000.00
	Being: electricity expense to 30 June		

This entry increases the electricity expense, which is an income tax deduction. However, you will need to reverse this entry in the new year in order to correctly account for the electricity account when it is subsequently paid:

1 July	Accrued expense	2000.00	
	Electricity		2000.00
	Being: reversal of the electricity expense to 30 June		

The accrued expense liability account is now zero, and when you pay the electricity account the $3000 debited to that account will be offset against the $2000 credit adjustment, leaving only the $1000 balance for the current year.

Many accounts, such as electricity, telephone and gas, give rise to an accrued expense adjustment, but such adjustments can only be done once the account has been received, often some weeks after the end of year. Such adjustments are tax effective for income tax provided that you are operating under an accruals regime.

Accrued expenses 2—leave entitlements

There are two parts to this topic:

▶ outstanding superannuation guarantee contributions as at 30 June

▶ other salary/wage and leave entitlements.

The 9 per cent superannuation guarantee paid quarterly by employers on behalf of their employees is not usually due until 28 July for wages and salary payments made up until 30 June. However, most computerised accounting systems make allowance for this and automatically create an accrued expense item. It is only when you calculate pays manually or perhaps through an agency that you need to consider the consequences of this timing difference.

If you only calculate and record your super payments as they fall due, in this case on 28 July, you will have to make an accrued expense adjustment as at 30 June to account for the superannuation contributions due as at 30 June but not payable until after the end of year.

> 30/6   Superannuation contribution (expense)
>   Accrued superannuation expense (liability)

As in the accrued expenses you will need to reverse this entry in the new year. Like other accrued expenses, the superannuation adjustment is a tax deductible expense.

The other side of this topic is the accounting adjustments required to employees' leave entitlements that have accrued as at year's end. A tax deduction is only available for leave amounts actually paid and therefore the following adjustments are not tax effective. You must ensure that your tax agent is aware of these adjustments before they calculate your income tax liability.

Annual leave

Employment conditions are governed by a combination of industrial awards, enterprise agreements or individual contracts. All full-time employees in Australia are entitled to a minimum of four weeks (20 working days) **annual leave** per year. This gives rise to an absolute obligation of accrued annual leave at year's end, although it is not a tax deduction until it is paid.

At year's end calculate the annual leave accrued entitlements for all your employees and cost it at their pay rate as at year's end.

Let us assume that this figure is $5567. You then adjust your annual leave expense for this provision:

Annual leave (expense)	5567.00	
Provision for annual leave (liability)		5567.00

Being: annual leave accrued at year's end

If you make this adjustment in the worksheet then your annual reports will reflect the correct position but you will not have to make any further adjustments to your accounting records. However, if you make this adjustment in your accounts, or your payroll system does this for you, then as annual leave is taken it will be written off against the annual leave provision and not recorded as an expense. You will have to be aware that a tax adjustment is required next year to account for this expense as a tax deduction.

Long service leave

This adjustment is the same as for annual leave. Most employees will be entitled to **long service leave** after 15 years, but many have an entitlement to be paid out after 10 years of service. Where any employee has an entitlement this should be reflected in the accounts:

Long service leave (expense)

Provision for long service leave (liability)

Being: long service leave accrued at year's end

Personal leave

Personal leave is the name given to a collection of leave entitlements such as sick leave and carer's leave. This type of leave, usually 10 days per year, accumulates year by year but is lost when an employee terminates their employment. Again you must determine the amount of this type of leave that has accumulated as at year's end and make the appropriate provision. However, not all of this leave type will be used so you should make a reasonable judgement about the amount of the accrued leave type that you believe, based on past performance, will actually be paid out and make the provision for this lesser amount:

> Personal leave (expense)
>> Provision for personal leave (liability)
>> *Being:* reasonable proportion of personal
>> leave accrued at year's end

Other leave types

Often the award agreement will give an employee an entitlement to other non-accumulating leave types such as study leave, compassionate leave and jury duty. No provision is required if these leave types are non-accumulative.

Prepaid income — income received in advance

Business owners often receive a deposit or perhaps a lay-by. These amounts are usually held in a liability account until the actual sale is completed, when they will be classified as income. However, the accounting and tax treatment of these amounts at year's end is a little more complex. The question you must ask yourself is, 'If a sale or contract is not completed, am I required to refund the advances held?' If the answer is yes, then the amounts are held on trust until the sale or service is supplied when it becomes income for both accounting and tax purposes. If you do not have to refund the monies, then the amounts deposited should be treated as income upon receipt. Any amounts held as non-refundable deposits should be classified as income at year's end and then reversed at the start of the new year.

The other common type of prepaid income is rent. If rent is received in advance and is across year's end, then that amount is apportioned across each income year. Let us assume that we receive $3300 for three months' office sub-let rent in advance on 1 May. As at 30 June, only $2200 applies to the current year and $1100 applies to the following year.

When we received the rent we classified it as income:

1/5	Operating bank account	3300.00	
	Rental income		3000.00
	GST		300.00
	Being: office rent received		

As at 30 June we need to move $1000 ($1100 net of GST) into prepaid rent, which is a liability account. It is not accounted for as income for either tax or accounting purposes:

30/6	Rental income	1000.00	
	Prepaid income (liability)		1000.00
	Being: rent for July to account for next year		

On 1 July we must reverse this entry and account for the prepaid rent as income in the new year:

1/7	Prepaid income (liability)	1000.00	
	Rental income		1000.00
	Being: rent for July received in advance last year		

Prepaid expenses

If you are using cash accounting and have prepaid an expense for less than 12 months, no adjustment is necessary. Under the accruals regime all 'material' prepayments must be adjusted.

The easiest prepayment to discuss is insurance. For example, if we pay our annual insurance account of $13 200 on 21 December to cover the period 1 January to 31 December, our journal entry will look like:

21/12	Insurance expense	12 000.00	
	GST	1 200.00	
	Bank		13 200.00
	Being: insurance for the period 1/1 to 31/12		

Ignoring the GST, the insurance expense represents $6000 for the current year and $6000 for our next financial year. Therefore we must adjust our insurance expense account by $6000:

30/6	Prepaid expenses (asset)	6000.00	
	Insurance expense		6000.00
	Being: insurance for next financial year		

On 1 July we need to reverse this in order to establish the expense account balance for the new year:

1/7	Insurance expense	6000.00	
	Prepaid expenses (asset)		6000.00
	Being: insurance for the period 1/7 to 31/12		

This is both an accounting and a tax effective adjustment to be made in your accounting records. These amounts should be known before the close of the period and therefore a journal adjustment on the last day of the financial year should be possible.

Prepayments — alternative treatment

One of the problems of prepaid expenses is that if the amount is recorded on payment against its appropriate account code, then there is a big jump in the expense payments for that month and an under-reporting of expenses for subsequent months. If you are monitoring your expenses on a month-to-month basis, as you would under a management budget, then this will cause significant problems.

One way to overcome this problem is to record all prepaid expenses into the prepaid expense asset account, then to make a journal entry adjustment at the beginning of each month.

The traditional recording of the insurance expense is:

21/12	Insurance expense	12 000.00	
	GST	1 200.00	
	Bank		13 200.00
	Being: insurance for the period 1/1 to 31/12		

The alternate treatment is:

21/12	Prepaid expenses (asset)	12 000.00	
	GST	1 200.00	
	Bank		13 200.00
	Being: insurance for the period 1/1 to 31/12		

Every month you then allocate that month's insurance expense to the appropriate account:

1/1	Insurance expense	1000.00	
	Prepaid expenses (asset)		1000.00
	Being: insurance for January		

1/2	Insurance expense	1000.00	
	Prepaid expenses (asset)		1000.00
	Being: insurance for February		

And so on for each month. When you do your monthly budget comparisons, the expense figure truly reflects the expenses for the period.

At the end of the year, all of this year's expense has been accounted for but the outstanding amount for next year is still in the prepaid expenses (asset) account, alleviating the need for any end-of-year adjustments.

This treatment takes a bit more work and close monitoring but provides a much better result, especially in the budgeting context.

End-of-period accounting

Two categories of adjustments have been outlined so far — those that are tax effective and those that are not. All of the adjustments in your accounting system should be done in period 13 so that your last month (period 12) contains only the transactions that relate to that month and is not corrupted with adjustment data. Any reversals should be done in period 0 if it is available, or period 1 if it is not.

Adjustments that are tax effective are:

▶ bad debt write-off as at the date the debt went bad

▶ end-of-year closing stock adjustments under the periodic system

▶ deprecation adjustments

▶ accrued income (if a legally enforceable debt)

▶ accrued expenses non-leave

▶ accrued expenses superannuation guarantee

▶ prepaid income — treated as income when received (if non-refundable)

▶ prepaid expenses.

Adjustments that are not tax effective are:

▶ provision for doubtful debts if required

▶ accrued expenses leave.

Closing off the books

The end-of-year process determines the profits for the period and zeroes off all of the income and expense accounts, starting the new year afresh. The asset, liability and equity accounts, on the other hand, start the new year with an opening balance that is the same as the last year's closing balance. This is a golden rule of accounting—last year's closing balance must equal this year's opening balance.

If you are using a computerised accounting program then the close-off of this year's accounts and the rollover of the opening balances into next year is an automated process. However, if you are using a manual system then you need to take the following steps.

The trading account

Create a new account called a trading account. This is known as a suspense or working account because it holds the balances of the income and cost of sales accounts only until the trading profit has been determined.

Close off each income account to the trading account. For example, you might have a sales account with a closing balance as at 30 June of $358 780. The journal entry that is required is:

30/6   Sales revenue   358 780.00
             Trading account   358 780.00
             Being: transfer of the
             closing balance to the
             trading account

The sales income account will now have a zero balance and is now ready for the new year. The trading account is now holding the income balance, as shown in table 4.1.

Table 4.1: trading account balances

Sales revenue   **5-1000**

Date	Particulars	Debit	Credit	Balance
30/06/YY	Sales to date		355 780	(355 780)
30/06/YY	Accrued Income		3 000	(358 780)
30/06/YY	Balance to trading	358 780		0

Trading account   **9-1000**

Date	Particulars	Debit	Credit	Balance
30/06/YY	Sales revenue		358 780	(358 780)

Likewise, close off all of your revenue and cost of sales accounts to the trading account until it looks something like table 4.2 (overleaf).

Table 4.2: close off revenue and cost of sales accounts

Trading account   9-1000

Date	Particulars	Debit	Credit	Balance
30/06/YY	Sales revenue		358780	(358780)
	Sales returns	567		(358213)
	Rental income		12000	(370213)
	Opening stock	23568		(346645)
	Purchases	108724		(237921)
	Inwards freight	45990		(191931)
	Closing stock		28887	(220818)
	To profit and loss account	220818		0

After all of the sales and cost of sales balances have been transferred in you can determine the trading profit amount. You then create another suspense account called a profit and loss account and journal the trading profit over to that account. If you do not have any cost of sales—that is, you are not a trading organisation—then you can skip over the trading account and use only the profit and loss account, shown in table 4.3.

Table 4.3: profit and loss account

Profit and loss account   9-2000

Date	Particulars	Debit	Credit	Balance
30/06/YY	Trading profit		220818	(220818)

You now journal in all of your other expense accounts leaving them with zero balances, as shown in table 4.4.

Table 4.4: expense accounts

Profit and loss account   **9-2000**

Date	Particulars	Debit	Credit	Balance
30/06/YY	Trading profit		220818	(220818)
	Advertising	4765		(216053)
	Depreciation	8100		(207953)
	Electricity	10234		(197719)
	Insurance	12000		(185719)
	Rent	10567		(175152)
	Staff leave	32378		(142774)
	Staff wages	112678		(30096)
	To retained earnings	30096		0

Your net profit figure of $30096 is now journalised into your retained earnings account and added to any outstanding balance in that equity account, as shown in table 4.5.

Table 4.5: retained earnings account

Retained earnings account   **3-3000**

Date	Particulars	Debit	Credit	Balance
30/06/YY	Current balance			(5233)
30/06/YY	Net profit ex P&L		30096	(35329)

You have now rolled over your books. All of your sales accounts are zero, the balances having been journalised to the trading account. The cost of sales accounts likewise are now all zero, the expense account has been zeroed off to the profit and loss account, and the final profit figure is now in the retained earnings equity account.

However, all of your asset, liability and equity accounts retain their closing 30 June balances as the opening 1 July balances. Under the running balance ledger format there is no need to do any further entries, but if you are using **T-accounts** then you will need to formally close them off and create the 1 July opening balances.

End-of-year accounting reports

Print the trading account, profit and loss account and a trial balance. It is from these documents that you will create the two fundamental reports required:

▶ statement of financial performance (usually known as the income statement)

▶ statement of financial position (usually known as the balance sheet).

The income statement

The income statement is a combination of the trading and profit and loss accounts. The information is set out in what is known as narrative style, as shown in table 4.6 and figure 4.1.

Table 4.6: trading account and profit and loss account

Trading account   9-1000

Date	Particulars	Debit	Credit	Balance
30/06/YY	Sales revenue		358 780	(358 780)
	Sales returns	567		(358 213)
	Rental income		12 000	(370 213)
	Opening stock	23 568		(346 645)
	Purchases	108 724		(237 921)
	Inwards freight	45 990		(191 931)
	Closing stock		28 887	(220 818)
	To profit and loss account	220 818		0

Profit and loss account   **9-2000**

Date	Particulars	Debit	Credit	Balance
30/06/YY	Trading profit		220818	(220818)
	Advertising	4765		(216053)
	Depreciation	8100		(207953)
	Electricity	10234		(197719)
	Insurance	12000		(185719)
	Rent	10567		(175152)
	Staff leave	32378		(142774)
	Staff wages	112678		(30096)
	To retained earnings	30096		0

Figure 4.1: sample income statement

Income statement for the period ended 30 June YY

Revenue

Sales	358780	
Less returns	567	358213
Rent income	12000	370213

***Less* cost of sales**

Opening inventory	23568	
Plus purchases	108724	
Inwards freight	45990	
Goods available for sale	178282	
Less closing stock	28887	149395
Trading or gross profit		220818

Figure 4.1: *(cont'd)*

Income statement for the period ended 30 June YY		
Less expenses		
Advertising	4765	
Depreciation	8100	
Electricity	10 234	
Insurance	12 000	
Rent	10 567	
Staff leave	32 378	
Staff wages	112 678	190 722
Net profit		**30 096**

The balance sheet

The balance sheet is the trial balance as at the close of the year once the sales, cost of sales and expenses have all been rolled over. The only balances left are the assets, liabilities and equity accounts, as shown in table 4.7 and figure 4.2.

Table 4.7: trial balance

Trial balance as at 30/6/YY

Detail	Debit	Credit
Bank account	7 942	
Inventory	28 887	
Accrued income	3 000	
Prepayment	6 000	
Car	25 000	
Accumulated depreciation		18 000
Truck	68 000	

Trial balance as at 30/6/YY

Detail	Debit	Credit
Accumulated depreciation		39 500
Trailer	12 000	
Accumulated depreciation		11 100
Accrued expenses		2 000
Provision for leave		5 567
Business loan		52 678
Capital		12 000
Drawings	25 345	
Retained earnings		35 329
	176 184	**176 174**

Figure 4.2: sample balance sheet

Balance sheet as at 30 June YY			
Assets			
Current assets			
Bank account	7 942		
Inventory	28 887		
Prepaid expenses	6 000		
Accrued income	3 000		45 829
Noncurrent assets			
Car	25 000		
Less acc. depreciation	18 000	7 000	
Truck	68 000		
Less acc. depreciation	39 500	28 500	
Trailer	12 000		
Less acc. depreciation	11 100	900	36 400
Total assets			**82 229**

Figure 4.2: *(cont'd)*

Balance sheet as at 30 June YY			
Liabilities			
Current liabilities			
Accrued expenses	2 000		
Provision for leave	5 567		7 567
Noncurrent liabilities			
Business loan			52 678
Equity			
Capital		12 000	
Retained earnings	35 329		
Less drawings	25 345	9 984	21 984
Total liabilities			**82 229**

Assets and liabilities are divided into current and noncurrent. A current asset will return a benefit to the business in the next accounting period (12 months), whereas a noncurrent asset, often called a fixed asset, is one that will provide a benefit over a longer term. A current liability requires servicing within the next accounting period (12 months), but a noncurrent liability is a long-term debt.

The layout of the accounts in this example is total assets = total liabilities (external liabilities plus equity), or in the form of the balance sheet equation A = L + E. This is the preferred layout under IFRS, whereas the traditional Australian layout is assets – liabilities (net assets) = equity, or A – L = E.

Revision exercise for day 4

Create an income statement and balance sheet in narrative form using the following information and trial balance.

Detail	30 June	
	Debit	Credit
Bank account	35 009	
Inventory	28 887	
Accounts receivable	3 225	
Accrued income		
Prepayment		
Car	25 000	
Accumulated depreciation		18 000
Truck	68 000	
Accumulated depreciation		39 500
Trailer	12 000	
Accumulated depreciation		11 100
Income in advance		
Accrued expenses		
Provision for leave		
Accrued wages		
Business loan		52 678
Capital		12 000
Drawings	35 500	
Retained earnings		9 984
Sales revenue		459 234

Detail	30 June	
	Debit	Credit
Sales returns	1 245	
Rental income		9 800
Opening stock		
Purchases	162 562	
Inwards freight	35 123	
Closing stock		
Gross or trading profit		
Advertising	5 678	
Depreciation		
Electricity	13 874	
Insurance	18 000	
Rent paid	12 500	
Staff leave	22 807	
Staff wages	132 886	
Net profit		
	612 296	612 296

1   The 30 June stocktake figure was $35 897.

2   Depreciate the PPE as follows:

    Car   2700

    Truck   4200

    Trailer   300

3   You received $1400 in rent that relates to the next financial year.

4   Your annual insurance account, paid on 20 December,
    covered the period 1 January to 31 December and was
    recorded against insurance expense for $7800.

5   Staff wages accumulated but not paid to 30 June
    were $2312.

6   Staff accrued leave was $23483.

Day 5

Cash and controls

Key terms and concepts

▶ *Archive:* a place where historical documents are stored.

▶ *Cash:* includes hard currency, cheques and electronic transfers.

▶ *Internal controls:* procedures that ensure all aspects of the business are authorised and conducted in accordance with company procedures.

▶ *Petty cash:* small amount of expenditure in hard currency, such as money used to buy coffee and milk for staff.

▶ *Phantom employees:* details recorded for an employee who does not exist; often past employees' details that have not been removed on termination.

▶ *Cash sales summary:* a breakdown of the day's sales into type and GST that reconciles with the till total sales and the bank deposit slip.

What is meant by cash?

In the days of the Romans, cash meant the coins in your purse. The British Empire introduced the concept of paper currency and, later, bills of exchange, the most common form today being the cheque. The 1970s saw the acceptance of a paperless cash transfer in the form of credit cards, which spawned the concept of direct debit.

Since the arrival of the internet, the term 'cash' has been widened to include all forms of electronic transfers such as paying bills online and the ability to pay accounts by direct transfer. An accountant calls these types of transactions cash and they need special consideration to prevent employee fraud. Yes, it can happen to you!

Many small business owners discount the possibility of fraud because they are hands-on with all aspects of the business. However, small businesses have a tendency to grow and if cash and other fraud prevention controls are not in place from day one, you will eventually be at risk.

Controls over cash

The monthly bank reconciliation procedure is one of the most fundamental internal controls over your cash position, but there are a number of other procedures and processes that must also be in place.

The float

One of the most basic controls over cash receipts is the float. A float is the amount of money in your till drawer at the beginning of the day so the cashier can give change for the first transactions of the day. At the end of the day the amount in the till drawer should equal the amount of sales shown on the till summary, often called a Z total, plus the float. For example, if you started the day with a $150 float and the till summary shows sales of $1523.52 for the day, then your cash drawer should contain $1673.52.

A few basic rules should be enforced to ensure that this control works. First, only one person should be in charge of the till at any one time. No-one else, including the owner or manager of the company, should be allowed anywhere near that till. At the end of the day the cashier is held responsible for reconciling the till drawer to the till Z total and recording the results on a cash sales summary (CSS) for **posting** into the cash receipts journal. The bank deposit slip can now be written up and that total must equal the total of the CSS for the day. If this is not the case your bank reconciliation will not work! This process is known as the daily close off. This leads us to a few procedural points.

▶ Under no circumstances is anyone to take cash out of the till. This rule must be strictly enforced, mainly against the business owners who are the worst culprits.

▶ All receipts must be banked daily and intact.

▶ Any deficiency in the till total is to be made up by the cashier, any surplus is to be banked as a business receipt.

Daily banking

Always bank your cash receipts daily, usually the next business day. Where this is not possible prepare a bank deposit for each day's receipts and bank them on a regular basis. Only very small businesses would modify this rule.

How can your staff close off after the end of the business day and still leave work on time? The answer is that the 'end of day' for most businesses is 3 pm, so you close off your till at 3 pm and remove the cash drawer, replacing it with a new drawer containing only the next day's float. All sales from 3 pm onwards are considered to be the next day's sales. Your cashier or assistant can now count and reconcile the cash and make up the CSS and bank deposit ready for banking the next day.

Your CSS will have to not only break down sales into category and the GST, but also the receipts into electronic transactions (debit and credit cards) and cash so that the cash component of the CSS can be reconciled against the bank deposit slip.

Petty cash

You may need a small amount of cash for some purpose, such as to buy a carton of milk for staff coffee. Do not take this money from the till. These small amounts of cash are handled under the petty cash **imprest system**, which is the universally accepted method of dealing with the small or **petty cash** needs of a business, irrespective of its size.

Buy a petty cash box or cash drawer and appoint one of your staff members (often the receptionist or cashier) as the petty cash custodian. The cash box should be locked when not in use. Ideally, there should be only one key, so that only one person is responsible for balancing and taking money out of the box. The cash box should be placed in a locked desk or file cabinet for further security when the user leaves the area or overnight. The location of the box should be kept as secret as possible.

The next step is to draw a cheque to cash for a petty cash float (let us assume it is for $200). The petty cash custodian cashes the cheque and places the money in the petty cash box. The cash journal will show a credit against your operating bank account and a debit to an asset account called petty cash, usually grouped with your other bank accounts. The petty cash account is an asset that represents the float amount and will not be used again unless you decide to increase or decrease the float.

When a staff member needs a small amount of cash for any purpose they spend their own money and obtain a receipt. The staff member then gives the receipt to the petty cash custodian who reimburses the expense. The amount of cash plus receipts in the box always adds up to the original float amount.

It is also common practice for the staff member to fill in a petty cash voucher when claiming the reimbursement (a sample voucher is shown in figure 5.1). The voucher details the nature of the expenditure for accounting purposes and is signed by the staff member as proof of receipt of the reimbursed cash. Some amounts in excess of a base limit, or for unusual purchases, may require authorisation which also appears on the voucher.

Figure 5.1: sample petty cash voucher

J Simms & Co. Petty cash reimbursement voucher	
Date:	Number:
Paid to:	
Reason:	
Account charge code:	
Amount:	GST included:
Signed as received:	Authorised by:

The petty cash accounting process

The petty cash custodian has a petty cash book into which all of the petty cash dealings are entered, as shown in table 5.1 (overleaf).

Table 5.1: petty cash dealings

Date	Voucher	Details	In	Out	Balance	GST	Staff	Stationery	MV	Other

The petty cash custodian enters into the petty cash book the details of the cash received through the initial float or subsequent reimbursements and also all of the amounts paid out. The balance at all times is the cash balance in the petty cash box.

For example, assume the following transactions:

1 Jan	Petty cash float of $200 created
2	$22 paid for petrol
3	$2.50 paid for milk
4	$33 paid for newspapers
5	$6.60 paid for biscuits for the canteen
6	$55 paid for staff overtime meals
7	$44 paid for new toner cartridge

The petty cash book is written up as shown in table 5.2.

Eventually the petty cash balance will need to be replenished. The petty cash custodian seeks reimbursement of the amounts paid out by completing a petty cash reimbursement claim form, or by photocopying the petty cash book pages and attaching all of the vouchers for the period. The total of the vouchers should equal the total of the reimbursement claim, as shown in table 5.3 (on p. 122).

Table 5.2: sample petty cash book

Date	Voucher	Details	In	Out	Balance	GST	Staff	Stationery	MV	Other
1 Jan			200.00		200.00					
2	1	Petrol		22.00	178.00	Y			22.00	
3	2	Milk		2.50	175.50	N	2.50			
4	3	Papers		33.00	142.50	Y				33.00
5	4	Canteen		6.60	135.90	Y	6.60			
6	5	Overtime meals		55.00	80.90	Y				55.00
7	6	Toner		44.00	36.90	Y		44.00		

Table 5.3: reimbursing petty cash

Date	Voucher	Details	In	Out	Balance	GST	Staff	Stationery	MV	Other
1 Jan			200.00		200.00					
2	1	Petrol		22.00	178.00	Y			22.00	
3	2	Milk		2.50	175.50	N	2.50			
4	3	Papers		33.00	142.50	Y				33.00
5	4	Canteen		6.60	135.90	Y	6.60			
6	5	Overtime meals		55.00	80.90	Y				55.00
7	6	Toner		44.00	36.90	Y		44.00		
8		Reimburse	163.10		200.00		9.10	44.00	22.00	88.00

The accountant uses the claim form as the source document to authorise the drawing of a cash cheque for the reimbursement amount. The cheque is drawn against the various expense codes as shown on the vouchers and detailed in the petty cash book, such as GST, staff amenities and motor vehicle expenses. Table 5.4 shows how the reimbursement appears in the journal entry.

Table 5.4: journal entry for reimbursement

Date	Particulars	Folio	Debit	Credit
8 Jan	Staff amenities	6-5670	2.50	
	Staff amenities	6-5670	6.00	
	Stationery	6-4560	40.00	
	Motor vehicle	6-3500	20.00	
	Miscellaneous	6-9000	80.00	
	GST	2-9900	14.60	
	Cash	1-1000		163.10
	Being: petty cash reimbursement			

The miscellaneous account is one of the few times that a non-specific account is acceptable. It is used for those minor items of little impact to the business paid through the petty cash system. Some businesses use this account for all petty cash expenditure, but it should only be used for truly miscellaneous items for which there is no current account code.

When the petty cash custodian receives the cheque they cash it at the bank and record the details in the petty cash book. At this stage the petty cash box should contain no vouchers and the balance in the book and the physical content of the petty cash box should equal the original petty cash float amount.

Fraud—it will never happen to me!

The biggest fraud threat to a business is the manipulation of accounting records by employees. This can take many forms, two of the most common being false invoicing and non-existent (phantom) employees. For example, the payroll manager of a white goods company stole $20 million over 18 months using phantom employees and a senior officer with a fashion group stole $16.6 million through false invoicing. Fraud cases worth $132 million were prosecuted in Australian courts in the first six months of 2010 and that is just the tip of the iceberg!

Many of the frauds committed against small businesses occur because only one person deals with particular types of payments and they have the opportunity to create either false invoices or phantom employees. Employees who have sole responsibility for inventory, such as a trusted warehouse employee, are also a source of concern. For example, a warehouse foreman of a cigarette distributor would work late every Friday night. He would then take a carton of cigarettes from the centre of a stack and sell them from his boot at a local pub to fund his gambling addiction. He was only found out when he went on leave and his replacement rotated the stock.

Most companies that fall prey to internal fraud usually have never really considered it. The most dangerous period is when a small business expands from a situation where the owner is in direct control to where the owner no longer has day-to-day control and the company finances have become more specialised and complex. This time of expansion may see trusted employees put in a position of sole control over certain aspects of the company's operations, possibly without the owners realising the danger, and the potential for fraud then arises.

Internal controls

Preventing fraud requires you to examine the company's business procedures to ensure that one employee does not have absolute control over one aspect of the business. However, we should distinguish between responsibility and control. Responsibility refers to the performance of the employee, which is usually monitored. Control means being able to undertake your duties without any checks and balances in place.

An employee responsible for payroll produces a payroll report at the end of each payroll run to be reviewed and approved to prove their performance. An employee in control of payroll only has to ensure that everyone is paid. That situation allows for phantoms to enter the system.

Internal controls are procedures put in place to ensure that all aspects of the business are authorised and conducted in accordance with company procedures. The controls could be as simple as ensuring that all cheques have two signatures and that each signatory double-checks the documents supporting the payment for accuracy.

What to do if fraud occurs

Fraudulent or illegal conduct may override employment contract provisions, including notice of termination, but you cannot deduct suspected losses from your employee's entitlements. Your employee's pay, leave and superannuation entitlements are protected by law and even where you feel the fraud is a breach of trust that should be punished, you cannot take matters into your own hands. The fraud should be viewed as a legal matter and not as a personal affront. Often, just terminating employment on the spot is considered action enough, although you must have real evidence and not just suspicion or you may find yourself on the wrong side of an unfair dismissal action.

If you consider the action serious enough to involve the police then you should bear in mind that police action will result in charges being laid against your employee and more than likely a considerable amount of your time will be involved in the action. Police action does not deal with the recovery of assets or with compensation. These are civil matters between you and your employee.

One path that you may consider is that of the Tax Office. All income, whether it is legal or not, is subject to taxation. 'Dobbing in' your employee to the Tax Office may give you some degree of satisfaction, but again it will not result in any recovery of assets or compensation.

Internal cash control methods for small businesses

Small business owners can use simple internal control procedures to assign responsibilities and reduce the risk of fraud. Although some small business owners feel that internal controls are just for larger companies, it is the small business with limited cash flow that is likely to be most damaged by fraud. Owners who implement and consistently use good internal controls can be more comfortable knowing that the cash that belongs in the business stays in the business. Employees who know that an owner is paying attention and monitoring cash movements are less likely to try something dishonest.

When a business is just starting, the owner probably undertakes most of the money handling functions themselves. As the business grows the volume of tasks grows and the owner has to begin delegating responsibilities to employees. While it would be nice to think that all employees are trustworthy and responsible, a prudent employer will use internal controls—a set of checks and balances—to be certain that no employee is mishandling funds or acting in a manner that is not in the best interest of the business.

Internal control of cash

There are five methods of internal control for cash:

▶ establishment of responsibility

▶ segregation of duties

▶ documentation procedures

▶ physical, mechanical and electronic controls

▶ independent internal verification.

Cash control verifies the complete nature and accurate recording of all cash that is received as well as any cash disbursements that take place.

To fully understand cash control, it is helpful to understand what is meant by the term 'cash'. Along with referring to currency and coin, cash also includes all forms of financial exchange such as electronic funds transfer (EFT), credit card receipts and cheques. Essentially, any type of financial exchange that can be immediately negotiated for a fixed value qualifies as cash.

Cash control means competently managing all these types of financial instrument by maintaining an accurate tracking system that accounts for both receiving and disbursing the cash. Designing a cash control process is not difficult at all. A few basic elements are incorporated into the process regardless of where the cash control procedure is used.

First, all transactions related to cash must be documented and recorded immediately. With cash control, there is no use of the accrual method of accounting. Each cash receipt is recorded upon receipt, while each disbursement is entered at the time that the payment is released. The mode of documentation requires only some basic template that will record the necessary data such as a cash receipt form.

Next, solid cash control procedures require that only certain individuals may have access to the cash. This type of security serves two purposes. First, accountability is established for the way that the cash is managed. Second, the empowerment of two people to oversee cash control helps to ensure that important transactions can take place at any given time, even if one individual is unavailable for some reason.

Cash control demands that the documents related to the task are kept separate from the physical location of the cash. In other words, the accounting book that is used to record the cash transactions should not be kept in the safe with the currency, money orders and cheques. This simple precaution helps to ensure that the task of altering the physical evidence related to cash in hand is more difficult and so minimises the chances for theft to occur.

Internal controls for cash receipts

Managing the process of cash collection helps to reduce the chances of theft. Physical controls are an important part of the process.

Cash is the lifeblood of a business and it is also the easiest item to steal. It is necessary to take precautions against theft of cash at the point of receipt and disbursement.

Businesses need to adopt procedures that account for cash and identify the amount and source of each transaction. It is important that adequate physical safeguards exist for cash.

Cash should never be in sight, but should be kept in a locked safe or drawer and only accessed by approved personnel.

In a largely cash business, such as a restaurant or small shop, one of the challenges for owners is to verify that all cash collected actually goes in the register. If an employee sells an item and pockets the cash, how will the owner know? One method for getting sales rung in the register accurately is to make only one employee responsible for the till. When the register is totalled at the end of a shift, the employee who has been operating the register has to explain any shortages.

Standard internal control procedures call for the person who prepares the bank deposit and the person who takes the deposit to the bank to be different. For a small business with limited staff, this may be difficult. An alternative procedure is for the bookkeeper who prepares the deposit and takes it to the bank to present to the owner the sales records for the day with a bank deposit receipt attached. Now that banking transactions are available online almost instantly, the owner can also verify the deposit online.

Physical protection of cash receipts

When dealing with larger amounts of cash receipts, physical separation with a window or other barrier is preferred. Larger amounts of cash should be taken through the window and placed in a locked box or drawer especially designed for the purpose. The cash should be out of sight of the customer to reduce temptation.

The drawer or safe should be emptied at night, or even multiple times each day if possible. The cashier windows should also have an alarm or panic button, usually under the desk, so that in an emergency the alarm can be tripped easily and without alerting the person at the window.

Securing cash at the end of the day

Employees who transport cash should be aware of their environments. They should vary their routines when leaving the building to reduce the chances of robbery. When moving large amounts, employees should always be accompanied. Armed security guards should be considered if appropriate.

Internal controls for cash payments

In a traditional company structure, a department issues a properly signed purchase order before an order is placed with a vendor. In a small business the owner or another employee is likely to pick up the phone and place the order directly without a written purchase order. How does an owner verify that no-one orders goods without prior authorisation?

Once goods have been ordered and shipped, they must be paid for. If the bookkeeper writes the cheques for outstanding invoices and presents them to the owner for signature, the owner can review all invoices before signing the cheques. The owner can verify that the purchases are appropriate and necessary, that the vendor has charged the correct price, and that the owner is familiar with all the vendors and the type of goods or services they supply.

Many businesses use online payments. Depending on the bank or service a business uses, administrative staff may be able to enter payment transactions and place them on hold pending the electronic approval of the owner or cheque signer. In the absence of that type of system, the owner could review and approve proposed payments, have the staff member process the electronic payments, then follow up with a review of the bank account online to verify the payments and amounts.

Cash management

Cash management covers a number of functions designed to process receipts and payments in an organised and efficient manner. Administering cash assets today often makes use of a number of automated support services offered by banks and other financial institutions.

Debt management

Debt is part of doing business and, in the form of financial leverage, debt may be beneficial and even necessary. But debt carries a cost—interest—and it should be carefully managed.

Debtor management

If you deal in credit sales you will have debtors; that is, customers who owe the business money. These debtors have to be managed to ensure timely cash receipts for the business.

The 'standard' business rule is that debtors should not exceed 30 per cent of your overall sales and that you should restrict the number of large credit customers to a manageable level. However, some small businesses rely entirely on credit sales for their income and quite a few have more than 50 per cent of their income tied up in just one or two big clients. The trick is managing these clients.

The first and most important step is credit worthiness. Before you accept any client for a credit sale you must ensure that they are able to pay. A simple credit check, or better still a phone call to other suppliers dealing with this client, may save a lot of headaches later on. However, privacy legislation regulates the reporting of credit information about individuals by credit providers and credit reporting agencies. The legislation also prevents businesses trading customers' personal information with others. Go to <www.privacy.gov.au> for more detailed information.

Of course, in a sales organisation refusal of a client will cause angst to the salesperson who will lose the commission on the sale. One method of minimising this is to only pay commission on settlement of the debt and not on completion of the sale.

Monitor payments by debtors (credit clients) to ensure that they fall within the stipulated credit terms. However, be aware that some firms, especially government agencies, pay within their own guidelines rather than yours. Governments expect a net 30 days condition and will usually pay on a 45 day average. You should also be very careful of organisations that appear to be government agencies but are in fact working on government grants. If they fail to get this year's grant it is quite possible you will bear the pain! Another annoying trend is that those firms with the best ability to pay are often the worst offenders.

To monitor recoveries, produce a monthly report after the finish of month's end that details debtors who have failed to pay on time and how far overdue their payment is. This report is usually called an aged debtors summary. You must also have procedures in place for dealing with late payers; for example:

▶ more than seven days late—send an email as a friendly reminder

▶ more than 14 days—phone them and stress the urgency of the matter

▶ more than 30 days—advise in writing, email or fax, that they are now on COD (cash on delivery) terms until the account is settled in full

▶ more than 45 days—the manager visits the debtor to determine if there is an underlying cause for non-payment, such as customer dissatisfaction

▶ more than 60 days—start recovery action.

You may also consider giving a discount for early payment, such as a 2.5 per cent discount if paid within seven days, otherwise full payment will be expected within 30 days. This is often written on the invoice as 2.5 per cent in seven days/Net 30.

One of the hardest decisions that a business has to make is to put one of their major clients onto COD or to start recovery action. You must be steadfast in this or you will carry the burden for the poor financial performance of others that could even lead to your own collapse.

Record retention

The paperless office is still a long way off. Under both tax and accounting rules you must keep your records for at least five years and they must be accessible to GST and income tax inspectors on demand. The following information will help you with this requirement.

Step one—a good filing system

Businesses usually have fairly good systems for tracking their sales, especially their credit purchases and sales. Computer systems such as MYOB handle this side of your business for you. But it is the supporting documentation for cash receipts and cash payments where businesses fall down.

Every transaction entered into by your organisation should have a supporting document. These documents are called the source documents and are the basis for entries into your accounting records.

For cash receipts these documents could be daily till total reports, your CSS, a receipt you have given to a customer or a copy of a customer's account that has been settled. All of your cash receipt source documents should be filed together on a day-by-day basis. Together with your daily bank deposit, the total of these documents should be able to prove the daily deposits entering your bank account. Ask yourself this question — if the Tax Office GST auditor were to randomly select a particular deposit into your account, could you easily find the supporting source document? You should file each month's receipts in a separate file, with each day's receipt documents filed in their own separate section. If a deposit does not include its own remittance advice then a copy of your supporting document should be made and included in the file as proof.

For cash payments the source document *must* be a tax invoice. It is a Tax Office requirement that if you wish to claim the GST credit you must hold a tax invoice. However, there may be instances where you do not wish to file the original in your cash payments system, such as when you purchase an asset and wish to keep the original documents in your assets register file. In these cases you should keep a photocopy in your cash payments file and the original in the asset's own file. The cash payments file should be kept in strict payment order, preferably with the cheque number on the document as its reference. Each month's payments should be kept in its own separate file.

Step two — archiving and record retention

The storage of old accounting records is a major headache for most firms, but if you keep your files in order they will be in neat monthly parcels.

You should keep the current year's cash receipts and cash payments files on hand for easy reference, but annually you should archive the previous year files. This usually takes place about six months into the current year, which means you will have between six and 18 months of current data to hand at any time. Last year's files should be filed in close proximity for easy reference if required. The previous year file—files more than two and a half years old—can be moved offsite into a convenient archive area.

The law requires that you keep records for at least five years. It is often prudent to extend this a little so that you normally have up to seven years' data to refer to if needed. Therefore annually you will move last year's records into storage and the previous year into offsite archive. Files more than seven years old are destroyed.

If you adhere to this routine you will always be able to put your hand on any supporting document required and at the same time keep your accounting filing system under control.

Revision exercise for day 5

On 1 May Mr Brown created a petty cash float and drew a cheque for $300. The following claims for petty cash were made by staff:

2 May $27.50 for taxi fare

3        $33 for stationery

4   Mrs Brown demands $68 for a parking fine

5        $6.60 for coffee

6        $2.20 for newspapers

7        $48.40 for petrol

Write up the petty cash book for those expenses that you pay, then claim a reimbursement for the total expended. As the accountant, write up the general journal entry required for the reimbursement.

Day 6

Employing and paying staff

Key terms and concepts

▶ *Ordinary time earnings (OTE):* the amount on which your employer superannuation contributions are based made up of your 'normal' wage or salary components.

▶ *Gross income:* an amount that includes your OTE but to which is added all other taxable items.

▶ *Allowances:* amounts that make up your employee's wage paid for a specific purpose, such as a dirt or tool allowance. Allowances are treated according to their type: work related or income related.

▶ *Work-related expenses:* amounts reimbursed through the payroll system to compensate employees for work-related expenditure. They are not included in gross income for withholding tax purposes.

▶ *Pay-as-you-go (PAYG):* a system by which the amounts of tax you withhold from your employees' wages are transferred to the Tax Office through your quarterly business activity statement (BAS).

Today we examine the complexities of employing and paying staff. Calculating wages so your staff are correctly paid is one of the main areas of concern for small business proprietors and their concerns are not unfounded. The tax law associated with the correct calculation of taxes withheld from employees' wages is arduous. This day explains how to correctly calculate wages and salaries, as well as the necessary record-keeping requirements.

The legal requirements of employing staff

Before you can employee anyone you must register as an employer with the Tax Office for PAYG withholding tax. Your **business activity statement (BAS)** will then include a field called withholding tax where you include the amount of tax that you have withheld from your employees' wages. Irrespective of how often you pay your employees, you only return the amounts withheld to the Tax Office on your monthly or quarterly BAS. Withholding amounts include amounts you withhold from your employees' and directors' wages, as well as amounts withheld from contractors who cannot provide an **Australian business number (ABN)**.

You should also ensure that you have the correct level of cover of workers' compensation insurance (this is a legal requirement) and that your employees have the correct qualifications and accreditations for the work they are to undertake (these requirements are beyond the scope of this text).

Your new employee should fill in a tax file number (TFN) declaration form (see figure 6.1 on p. 140). If the employee fails to provide you with the completed form, then you must deduct 46.5 per cent tax from their net pay. This form provides you with all the information that you need to complete a wage or salary calculation, such as:

▶ the employee's TFN

▶ the employee's name and address

▶ whether the employee is an Australian tax resident

▶ whether the employee is claiming the **tax-free threshold**

▶ whether the employee has a **higher education loan program (HELP)** debt

▶ whether the employee has a financial supplement debt.

You complete your details, such as ABN and company name, on the second part of the form. Send the original form to the Tax Office within 14 days and keep a copy on the employee's file. You must also provide the employee's superannuation fund with the employee's TFN number.

Tax residency

Australians' liability to tax is based upon the concept of tax *residency*, not citizenship. Australian tax residents are generally taxed on their worldwide income, whereas non-residents are generally taxed only on their Australian-sourced income.

You are considered to be an Australian resident for tax purposes if you:

▶ have always lived in Australia or you have come to Australia to live

▶ have been in Australia for more than half of the income year (unless your usual home is overseas and you do not intend to live in Australia; for example, if you are a working holiday maker)

▶ are an overseas student enrolled in a course of study for more than six months.

Figure 6.1: tax file number declaration form

ORIGINAL – ATO copy

Australian Government
Australian Taxation Office

www.ato.gov.au

Tax file number declaration

This declaration is NOT an application for a tax file number.
- Use a black or blue pen and print clearly in BLOCK LETTERS.
- Print X in the appropriate boxes.
- Read all the instructions before you complete this declaration.

30920710

Section A: To be completed by the PAYEE

1 What is your tax file number (TFN)?

See Privacy of information on page 4 of the instructions.

OR I have made a separate application/enquiry to the ATO for a new or existing TFN.

OR I am claiming an exemption because I am under 18 years of age and do not earn enough to pay tax.

OR I am claiming an exemption because I am in receipt of a pension, benefit or allowance.

2 What is your name? Title: Mr Mrs Miss Ms

Surname or family name

First given name

Other given names

3 If you have changed your name since you last dealt with the ATO, show your previous family name

4 What is your date of birth? Day / Month / Year

5 What is your home address in Australia?

Suburb or town

State/territory Postcode

6 On what basis are you paid? (Select only one.) Full-time employment / Part-time employment / Labour hire / Superannuation income stream / Casual employment

7 Are you an Australian resident for tax purposes? Yes No — You must answer No at question 8.

8 Do you want to claim the tax-free threshold from this payer?

Only claim the tax-free threshold from one payer.

If you have more than one source of income and currently claim the tax-free threshold from another payer, do not claim it now.

Yes No — Answer no to questions 9 and 10 unless you are a non-resident claiming a senior Australian, zone or overseas forces tax offset.

9 Do you want to claim the senior Australians tax offset by reducing the amount withheld from payments made to you?

Yes — Complete a Withholding declaration (NAT 3093), but only if you are claiming the tax-free threshold from this payer. If you have more than one payer, see page 3 of the instructions. No

10 Do you want to claim a zone, overseas forces, dependent spouse or special tax offset by reducing the amount withheld from payments made to you?

Yes — Complete a Withholding declaration (NAT 3093). No

11 (a) Do you have an accumulated Higher Education Loan Program (HELP) debt?

Yes — Your payer will withhold additional amounts to cover any compulsory repayments. No

(b) Do you have an accumulated Financial Supplement debt?

Yes — Your payer will withhold additional amounts to cover any compulsory repayments. No

DECLARATION by payee: *I declare that the information I have given is true and correct.*

Signature — YOU MUST SIGN HERE — Date Day / Month / Year

There are penalties for deliberately making a false or misleading statement.

Once Section A is completed and signed, give it to your payer.

Section B: To be completed by the PAYER (if you are not lodging online)

1 What is your Australian business number (ABN) or your withholding payer number? Branch number (if applicable)

2 If you don't have an ABN or withholding payer number, have you applied for one? Yes No — See 'More information' on page 4 of the instructions.

3 What is your registered business name or trading name (or your individual name if not in business)?

4 What is your business address?

Suburb or town

State/territory Postcode

5 Who is your contact person?

Business phone number

6 If you no longer make payments to this payee, print X in this box

DECLARATION by payer: *I declare that the information I have given is true and correct.*

Signature of payer — Date Day / Month / Year

There are penalties for deliberately making a false or misleading statement.

Return the completed original ATO copy to:

For WA, SA, NT, VIC or TAS: Australian Taxation Office, PO Box 795, ALBURY NSW 2640

For NSW, QLD or ACT: Australian Taxation Office, PO Box 9004, PENRITH NSW 2740

IMPORTANT — See reverse side of PAYER's copy for: payer obligations; lodging online.

TAXPAYER-IN-CONFIDENCE (when completed)

NAT 3092-07.2010

Sample only

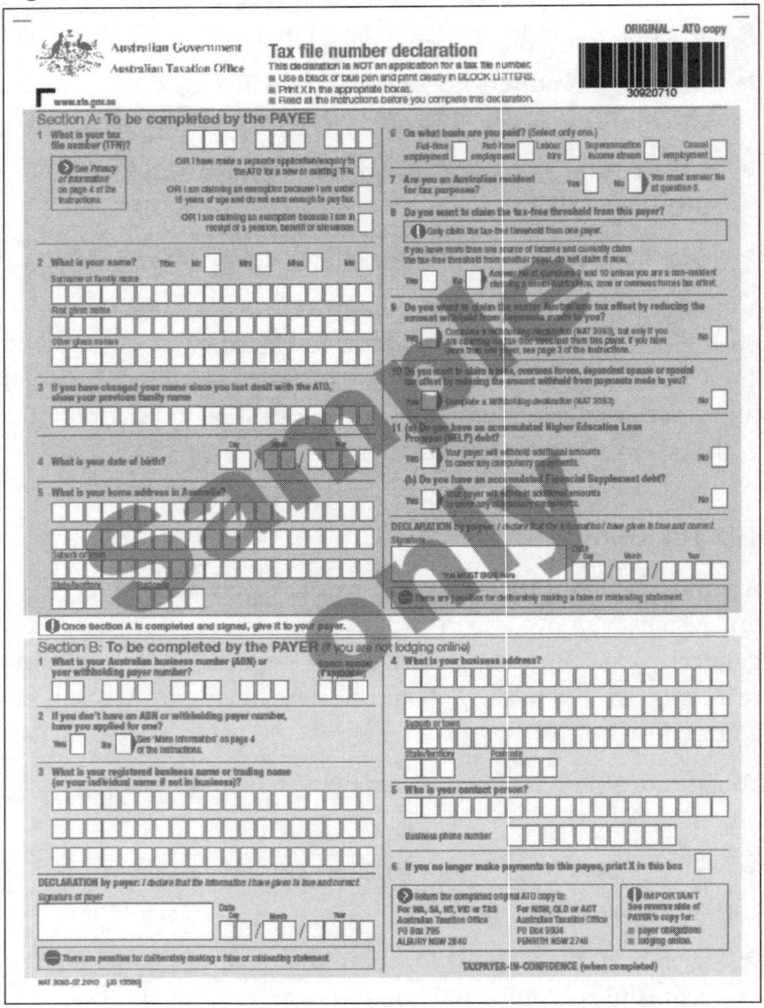

The tax rates that apply depend on whether or not you are an Australian resident. A higher rate of tax is applied to a non-resident's Australian income and non-residents are not entitled to a tax-free threshold. Non-residents also have limited access to Medicare and social security. Lower tax rates and the tax-free threshold apply to Australian tax residents, but they pay that tax on their worldwide income.

Tax-free threshold

Only Australian tax residents can claim the tax-free threshold of the first $6000 of their income. Employees can claim the tax-free threshold from only one employer each year, so if you are employing someone such as a casual and this is their second job, they may not be able to claim the tax-free threshold.

Higher education loan program

A higher education loan program (HELP) debt is money that the taxpayer borrowed from the federal government to subsidise their education. The debt is repaid through the tax system once the taxpayer income reaches a certain level ($44912 per annum for 2010). The percentage of tax applied starts at 4 per cent and rises as the income level increases to 8 per cent once your employee's annual income reaches $83408.

Financial supplement debt

This student loan scheme closed in 2003; however, some of your employees may still have an outstanding debt.

Employee requests

Employees may also require that you take into account a rebate to which they are entitled or to vary the tax rate that applies when calculating their tax. Such requests must be made in writing. If the employee wants to pay less tax, their request must be made through a Tax Office variation authorisation.

All of the processes mentioned so far can be completed using computer-based applications. If you have fewer than 10 employees, you can make the calculations manually using a tax calculator that can be downloaded from the ATO site. For more than 10 but fewer than 20 employees I strongly suggest that you use a payroll package such as MYOB. For more than 20 employees a payroll service is the way to go.

Wages and salaries

Wages are traditionally calculated on an hourly basis while a salary is a fixed amount per month or year. Casual rates are paid per hour of attendance and are usually higher than the rates paid to permanent employees. Some employees are paid by commission, or a base salary plus commission. Bonuses are often part of the salary package and in some instances may be an unexpected reward for good service.

Ordinary time earnings

Our first priority is to work out our employee's base wage or **ordinary time earnings (OTE)**. OTE include employees' earnings for ordinary hours of work as well as over-award payments, paid leave, commissions and shift allowances.

The first step is to calculate the two types of income, the OTE and the larger amount of gross income for tax purposes. Both of these amounts include an employee's base wage, but it is in the question of penalties and allowances where the differences apply.

Penalties and allowances

It is not unusual for an employee's entitlements to include amounts that are in addition to their base rate of pay. For instance, shift workers receive a penalty payment as compensation for working outside normal business hours and tradespeople often get a tool allowance for using their own tools on the job. Some allowances are not subject to tax and are not included in the wage calculations at all, such as reimbursement for business-related expenditure. Some allowances are included in both OTE and gross income, while others are included only in gross income.

Payments included in OTE and gross income include:

▶ 'normal' wages or salary for hours worked

▶ allowances for qualifications, such as first aid or safety qualifications

▶ allowances that are not reimbursement of expenses

▶ meals that are not part of the employment award, danger, dirt, height, shift and travelling time

▶ bonuses related to specific performance

▶ commissions

▶ over-award payments

▶ shift loading

▶ casual loading

▶ annual holiday leave taken

▶ sick leave taken

▶ long service leave

▶ government subsidies such as Job Start.

In addition to the payments listed above, the following payments are included in gross income:

▶ overtime

▶ allowances for tax deductible items

▶ uniform laundry of more than $150 per year, uniform dry cleaning, tools, motor vehicle paid over the tax rate or for non-deductible (private) use

▶ bonuses not related to specific performance, such as a Christmas bonus

▶ jury duty or reserve forces top-up payments

▶ maternity or paternity leave

▶ annual leave loading

▶ accrued leave paid on termination

▶ redundancy or payments in lieu of notice

▶ other payments paid on termination, such as severance pay.

Payments outside the wages tax calculation that are shown on the payslip and payment summary include:

▶ reimbursement for deductible business-related expenses, such as motor vehicle reimbursement within Tax Office guidelines, tool allowances and other work-related expenses

▶ an expense allowance paid in expectation that it will be fully expended for business-related purposes (any private use or retained surplus is taxable)

▶ workers' compensation payments including salary top-ups

▶ benefits paid that are subject to fringe benefits tax.

Payments outside the wages calculation that are shown on the payslip but not on the payment summary include:

▶ reasonable domestic travel costs

▶ reasonable amounts for meal allowances paid under an award ($24.95 for 2010).

Reasonable amounts for domestic travel and award meal allowances are published on the Tax Office website.

Allowances

Employees may be paid a variety of allowances.

Work-related expenses outside of wages tax calculation refers to the payment of an allowance for which the employee can claim a compensating deduction on their tax return. Therefore, as an employer you do not tax this allowance, but it must be declared on the employee's tax return and an offsetting deduction claimed. Any difference is taxable to the employee.

Annual leave loading is an additional 17.5 per cent loading (to a maximum of $320) paid to workers taking annual leave provided that such a leave loading arrangement is part of that worker's industrial award, for example cleaners. You must pay the 17.5 per cent annual leave loading calculated on the employees' ordinary time rate of pay, which is not the same as the ordinary times earnings for superannuation purposes but is an amount defined separately in each award. Employees entitled to a leave loading pay a slightly higher rate of tax throughout the year so that the amount of the loading is not taxed when it is taken.

If you are unsure of which award your workers fall under, contact the Department of Commerce for guidance.

Annual leave is paid time off that an employee usually uses for recreational purposes, such as to take a holiday. Full-time employees are entitled to four weeks of paid annual leave for every year that they work for your business. Part-time employees receive a pro rata amount of annual leave, which means a proportionate amount based on their hours of work.

Casual employees are not paid annual leave. If your business employs shift workers, they may be entitled to an additional week of annual leave every year. You and your employees need to agree on a time for them to take annual leave and you cannot 'unreasonably refuse' the request.

When an employee finishes working for your business, all of their unused annual leave must be paid out to them at the amount they would have received if they had taken the annual leave, including any leave loading.

Workers' compensation payments are outside of the wages system provided that the employee does not have to work to receive the payment. If the payment requires some form of work commitment then it is included in both OTE and gross income as a normal wage or salary.

Superannuation

Employees aged between 18 and 69 years who earn more than $450 per month must have 9 per cent of OTE paid into a complying superannuation fund (or retirement savings account) of their choice. It makes no difference whether the employee is employed full time or part time, or on a contract or casual basis, the employer must still contribute 9 per cent of their OTE to a super fund. If your employee is less than 18 years of age and works more than 30 hours per week, they are also eligible for a 9 per cent super contribution. The payments start from your employee's first pay, with a maximum salary applicable of $160,680 per year.

The payment must be made within 28 days after the end of each quarter for all salary and wage payments in that quarter. The payment of your employee's super contribution is deductible to the business, but only when it has been paid, not when it was accrued.

If you fail to provide these super payments for your employees you will receive a penalty: the superannuation guarantee charge. The penalty is based on the amount that should have been paid, an interest charge of 10 per cent plus an administration charge. The superannuation guarantee charge is a penalty so it is not tax deductible.

Putting it all together

Here is one example (the second example is on p. 160) that applies what you've learned so far in this day.

Example 1

You employ a tradesperson as a wages employee at $35 per hour. Alex provides her own van and tools and claims an allowance for the use of these. Overtime is in addition to normal wages.

For the pay fortnight Alex works nine eight-hour days and has one eight-hour day of sick leave. She works one Saturday morning for four hours overtime at time and one half. Her tool allowance is $50 per week and travel is paid at the tax rate of 60 cents per kilometre of work-related travel. She travelled 375 kilometres in the fortnight and has submitted a travel claim for the period.

What is her OTE, gross income for tax purposes and additional work-related payments?

Answer

OTE includes normal hours wages and sick leave:

Hours worked:	9 days × 8 hours @ $35	2520
Sick leave:	8 hours @ $35	280
		2800

Example 1 *(cont'd)*

Additional amounts included in gross income:

Overtime:	4 hours @ 1.5 at $35	210
		3010

Non-taxable business-related expenditure reimbursement:

Travel allowance:	350k at $0.60	210
Tool allowance:	2 weeks at $50	100
		3320

Superannuation is paid at 9 per cent of OTE and tax calculated on the total gross earnings. Non-taxable business-related expenses are not taxed as part of the PAYG system, but are included in the employee's own tax return along with an offsetting claim for a deduction for business-related expenditure.

Doing the calculations

Now that we have both OTE and gross earnings we can do the necessary calculations.

Superannuation contribution

The superannuation contribution is 9 per cent of OTE:

$$9\% \times \$2800 = \$252$$

The superannuation amount is shown on the payslip but is not included in any of the amounts payable. The journal entry to account for the superannuation contribution is:

Alex superannuation	252.00	
Superannuation expense		252.00

Each employee could have their own salary account and associated superannuation account as above so that you can track the individual payments as needed. Alternatively, you could keep the details separate in each employee's pay file, in which case the debit entry would be to a general salary and wage on-cost account rather than the individual's superannuation account.

Every quarter you pay out the superannuation amount to the individual employee's super fund. To facilitate this, set up a spreadsheet file with the employee's name, super fund and employee superannuation number. Some funds allow you to pay into their account electronically while others require a cheque and an accompanying schedule of contributions. A retirement savings account (RSA) that you can open with some banks to hold small amounts of superannuation payments may even require you to complete something similar to a bank deposit slip.

If you are a small business with fewer than 20 employees, then you can use the facility set up by the Australian government and administered by Medicare called the small business superannuation clearing house. This facility allows you to pay one bulk amount into an account with Medicare and have Medicare make the individual distributions for you. More information on this service can be found at <www.medicareaustralia.gov.au/super>

PAYG income tax

PAYG income tax is the crux of the whole payroll system. You can use six separate schedules to work out the amount of tax to be deducted from an employee's wage, including income tax, **Medicare levy** and HECS-type (student loan) repayments. Each of these schedules is available for weekly, fortnightly or monthly wage calculations. There are 18 separate schedules, each of which vary from year to year, so which one do you use?

There are three basic ways you calculate the tax that you must withhold: manually, using a payroll package such as MYOB, or using a payroll service. In the following example we use the manual system.

Fortunately the Tax Office makes the manual calculation a lot easier than using the traditional paper-based approach. If you go to the Tax Office site at <www.ato.gov.au> and type TWC into the search field it will bring up details for the tax withheld calculation application. Click 'Download the calculator' in the right side menu to download (save), then install (run) the calculator on your PC.

Enter the information into the TWC (see figure 6.2).

Figure 6.2: enter the information into the tax withheld calculation application

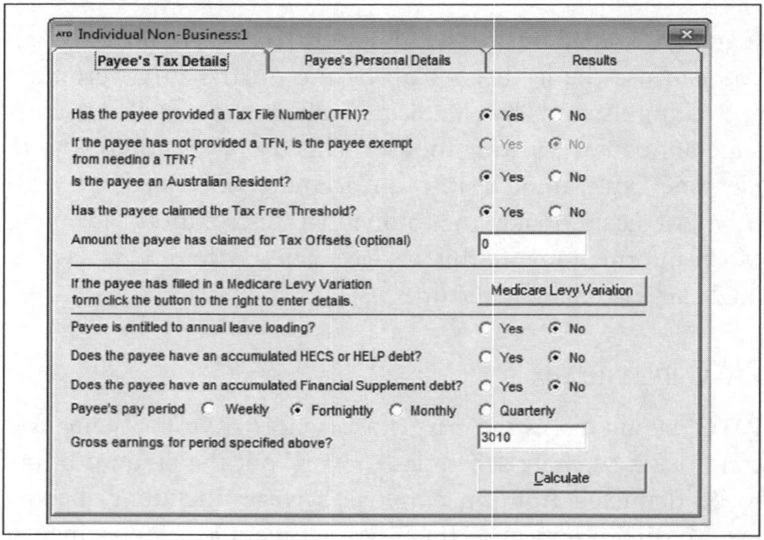

The result of entering the information is shown in figure 6.3.

Figure 6.3: the result of entering the information into the TWC

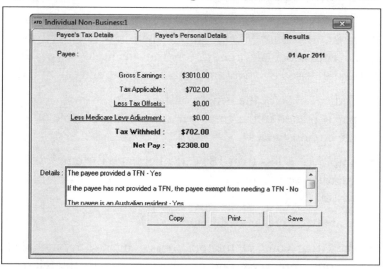

What could be easier? The tax on Alex's gross income is $702.

The next step is to create a payslip for Alex and enter the details into your accounting system, but before you do this you must consider any deductions that Alex may have requested (in writing) be made from her wage.

Employee deductions

According to Australia's Fair Work Ombudsman, an employer is allowed to make a deduction from an employee's pay if:

▶ the employee agreed in writing and the deduction is principally for the employee's benefit

▶ the employee authorised the deduction in accordance with an enterprise agreement

▶ the deduction is authorised by or under an award or an order of Fair Work Australia

▶ the deduction is authorised by or under a law or an order of a court.

However, the Fair Work Ombudsman also states that an employer cannot make a deduction from an employee's pay even if it is authorised by an award or an enterprise agreement if the:

▶ deduction is for the benefit of the employer or is partly related to the employer and is unreasonable in the circumstances

▶ employee is less than 18 years of age and the employee's guardian or parent hasn't authorised the deduction in writing.

There are two types of deductions:

▶ those that 'come off the top'; that is, they are not included in your employee's wage or salary and are usually referred to as salary sacrifice amounts

▶ deductions that you make from the after-tax net income amount.

You can only legally deduct amounts from an employee's wage where you hold that request from the employee in writing or it is covered as part of an award agreement. Employers cannot make ad hoc deductions from an employee's legal entitlement.

Salary sacrifice

There are three types of salary sacrifice.

The first is an amount of additional superannuation that the employee requests (in writing) be deducted each pay and sent, along with the usual 9 per cent employer contribution, to the employee's superannuation fund. Although legally this deducted amount does not have to be included in the OTE for the purposes of calculating the 9 per cent employer's contribution, it is normal business practice to do so. Superannuation can be deducted from an employee's wage before tax without incurring any fringe benefits tax (FBT) liability.

The second common type of pre-tax deduction is where an employee 'purchases' additional leave. This is in fact a leave-without-pay arrangement where wages are adjusted over time to account for the additional leave period. There are no tax implications in making such an arrangement and whether the amount is included in the employee's OTE is a matter of negotiation at the time that the employee applies to go onto the scheme.

The third but far less common deduction is where an employee requests that amounts of pre-tax wages be applied for their private use. This automatically triggers an FBT problem and therefore is not usually accepted by the employer, except in a few very specific circumstances. This is discussed in more depth in day 7 where FBT is discussed.

The payslip

Calculating gross income and OTE is a different process from that used to create the payslip. Every employee is entitled to receive a payslip, even if they are on leave, within one working day of the pay date. The payslip can be in hard copy form or electronic provided that the employee has access to, and can print a copy of, the electronic form. An increasing number of employers are using a PDF attachment to an email for this purpose.

The employee's payslip must include:

▶ the name of the employer (for example, XYZ Pty Ltd trading as XYZ Pie Shop)

▶ the Australian business number (ABN) of the employer

▶ the employee's name

▶ the date of payment

▶ the pay period (for example, 24/3/09 to 30/3/09)

▶ the gross and net amount of pay

▶ any loadings, monetary allowances, bonuses, incentive-based payments, penalty rates or other entitlements paid that can be singled out

▶ if the employee is paid an hourly rate, the ordinary hourly pay rate and number of hours worked at that rate and the amount of pay at that rate

▶ if the employee is paid an annual rate (salary), the rate as at the last day in the pay period

▶ any deductions made from your employee's pay, including the amount and details of each deduction (including superannuation) as well as the name, or the name and number, of the fund or account the deductions are paid into (see figure 6.4)

▶ if you are required to pay superannuation contributions for your employee's benefit, include:

  ⌑ the amount of each superannuation contribution made during the period to which the payslip relates, or the amounts of contributions that you are liable to make

  ⌑ the name or the name and number of the superannuation fund you put or will put superannuation contributions into.

Figure 6.4: pay deductions request

Alex requires us to pay her union dues of $35 per fortnight and her Medibank Private health cover of $55 per fortnight. She also requests that we deduct an extra $50 in income tax. All requests have been made in writing.

When you employ people under a modern award or agreement you are legally required to keep accurate and complete time and wages records and issue pay slips to each employee. You must keep all time and wages records of each employee for at least seven years. These records should be in plain English and easy to read.

Figure 6.5 is an example of a complete payslip. A sample payslip in Excel is available from my website <www.tpabusiness.com.au>.

Figure 6.5: a complete payslip

Big Daddy Electrical Contractors
22 Fairfield Crescent, Nowhere NSW 2789
ABN 1234 12345

Pay date   19/07/20Y1
Employee   Ms Alex Hanson
Pay period   01/07/20Y1 to 14/07/20Y1

Wages

Wages	9 days at 8 hours at $35.00	2520.00
Overtime	4 hours at 1.5	210.00
Sick leave	8 hours	280.00
		3010.00

Allowances

Tool allowance		100.00
Travel 350 k at $0.60		210.00
Gross pay		**3320.00**

Deductions

Income tax		702.00
Additional tax		50.00
Union dues	(Electrical Trades Union)	35.00
Medibank Private		55.00
Amount paid	**(ANZ ***345)**	**2478.00**

Leave details

Leave type	Annual entitlement	Opening balance (hrs)	Accrued (hrs)	Used (hrs)	Closing balance (hrs)
Annual leave	20 days	66.5	6.4	0	70.9
Sick leave	10 days	25.2	3.2	8	20.4

Superannuation
9% employer's contribution of $252.00 paid into ETU Superannuation

Employees are entitled to know the exact balance of their leave at all times. You must keep accurate and current records of all leave balances. The easiest way to do this in a small business with fewer than 10 employees is to keep a spreadsheet for each employee with their full details that you can cut and paste into a word processing document each payday.

Payday accounting

We have already accounted for superannuation, so now we analyse the payslip and categorise each entry into a general ledger account and a debit or credit amount, as shown in table 6.1. The memo or description for each entry should be the employee's name.

Table 6.1: categorising debits and credits

Description	Category	Dr	Cr
Wages	Wages	2520	
Overtime	Wages	210	
Sick leave	Wages	280	
Tool allowance	Wages	100	
Travel	M/V expense	210	
Income tax	Accrued income tax		702
Additional tax	Accrued income tax		50
Union dues	Accrued payables (staff deductions)		35
Medibank Private	Accrued payables (staff deductions)		55
Amount paid	**Wages bank account**		**2478**

The total of the wages and overtime appear on the BAS under gross income at W1. The total of accrued income tax is the amount that appears on the BAS under withholding taxes at W1 (totalled to W5 and transferred to summary item 4) and is cleared when you pay the BAS balance.

The accrued payables (staff deductions) account is cleared as you pay Alex's private medical insurance and union dues. Each of these organisations have their own method of accepting payments from employers and need you to quote the employee's own reference number for each organisation. Staff deducted amounts, other than superannuation and income tax that are paid quarterly and on the BAS respectfully, should be paid as soon as possible (the next working day) after payday.

Annual reporting requirements

It is a legal requirement that you provide each employee with a payment summary (which used to be known as a group certificate) within 28 days of the end of the financial year. This payment summary contains details of all payments you have made to the employee for the purpose of allowing the employee to complete their annual tax return.

However, the payment summary, a copy of which you forward to the Tax Office, is also used by the Tax Office to calculate other employee obligations such as child support. For this reason, it also contains information on payments made on the employee's behalf such as salary sacrifice amounts and employer payments that are subject to fringe benefits tax (referred to as reportable fringe benefit amounts). FBT is discussed at length in day 7.

PAYG payment summary forms and a set of instructions are available from the Tax Office (see figure 6.6, overleaf). The form is a three-part pre-carbonised form—the original is sent to the Tax Office, the second copy is for your employee and has employee instructions printed on the reverse, and the third copy is for your records, to be filed in the employee's pay file.

Figure 6.6: PAYG payment summary

Australian Government
Australian Taxation Office

PAYG payment summary – individual non-business

00461109

All sections of this form must be completed. For help, refer to *How to complete the PAYG payment summary – individual non-business* (NAT 3388).

If you are amending a payment summary you have already sent, place X in this box.

Payment summary for year ending 30 June

Section A: **Payee details**

Payee's surname or family name

Payee's given name/s

Payee's residential address

Suburb/town/locality · State/territory · Postcode

Date of birth (if known) Day / Month / Year

Section B: **Payment details**

Period during which payments were made Day / Month / Year to Day / Month / Year

Payee's tax file number

TOTAL TAX WITHHELD $ .00

Total tax withheld – whole dollars only in words

If the information on this payment summary relates to payments of a pension or annuity, place X in this box.

GROSS PAYMENTS (do not include amounts shown under 'Allowances', 'Lump sum payments', 'CDEP payments' and 'Exempt foreign employment income') $ .00

Community Development Employment Projects (CDEP) payments $ .00

Reportable fringe benefits amount FBT year 1 April to 31 March $ .00

Reportable employer superannuation contributions $ .00

Deductible amount of the undeducted purchase price of an annuity $ .00

Lump sum A $ .00 Type

Lump sum B $ .00

Lump sum D $ .00

Lump sum E $ .00

Exempt foreign employment income Amount $ .00

Allowances (provide details) $ .00

Total allowances $ .00

Union/Professional association fees – Name of organisation Amount $ .00

Workplace giving – Name of organisation $ .00

Tax Office original

Section C: **Payer details**

You must also complete this section

Payer's Australian business number (ABN) or withholding payer number (WPN) Branch number

Payer's name (use the same name that appears on your activity statement)

DECLARATION – *I declare that the information given on this form is complete and correct.*

Signature of authorised person

Date Day / Month / Year

NAT 0046-11.2009 JS 11695

Sample only

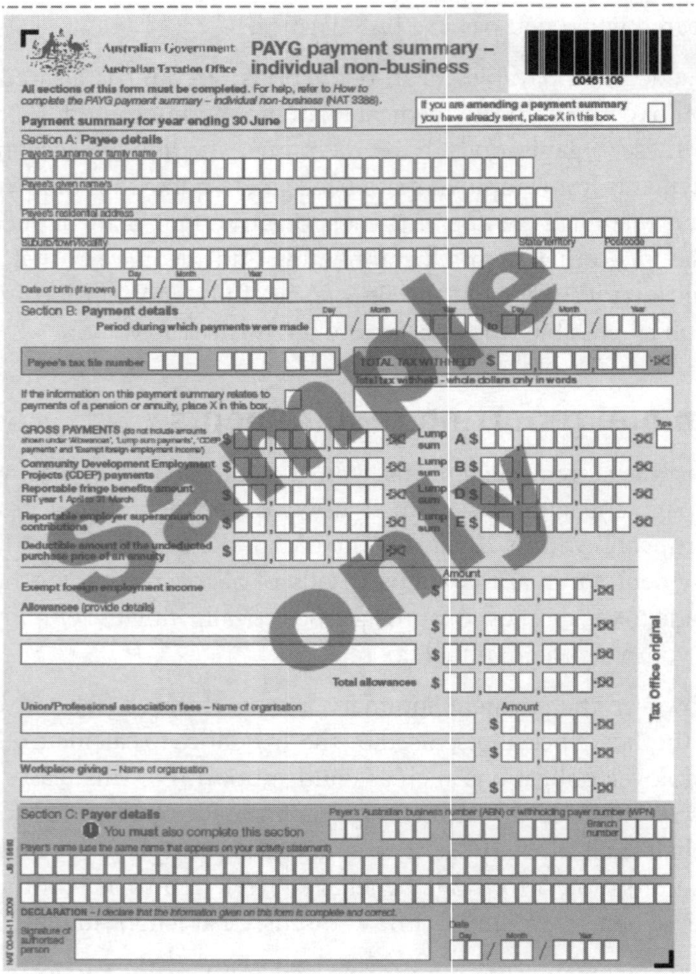

The payment summary is in three sections. Section A shows employee details such as name, address and date of birth, which are required for identification purposes. Section B contains payment details that we discuss below and section C is for the employer's name, ABN and signature to the declaration.

Section B, payment details, is where you enter the payroll information. Note that the amounts are entered in whole dollars only — ignore the cents.

You need to include the following information in section B:

▶ payment period — usually 1/7/Y1 to 30/6/Y2

▶ employee's TFN — as per the employee's TFN declaration

▶ total tax withheld — in dollars and words

▶ gross payments — includes the gross amount of all payments such as wages, salary, overtime, bonuses and commissions, as well as any outstanding leave balances paid on resignation

▶ reportable fringe benefits — certain FBT items of more than $2000 in total

▶ reportable employer superannuation — include any superannuation payments made over and above the 9 per cent superannuation contribution, such as salary sacrifice amounts

▶ allowances paid — for work-related expenses *not* included in the gross income amount, such as tool allowance and motor vehicle allowance. The payments must be shown in detail. If there is not enough room, report as 'various' and attach a detailed breakdown for each payment made.

▶ union/professional fees — the name and payment made to the association. This amount should be included in the gross income amount.

CDEP and annuity payments are included in section B but are beyond the realm of a normal small business employer–employee relationship.

Example 2

If the earlier payslip was the only payslip Alex received for the year, what would her annual payment summary contain?

PAYG payment summary

Section A	Payee details
Payee surname	Hanson
Payee given name	Alex
Payee address	123 Anywhere Street Nowhere NSW 3456
Date of birth	20/11/1985

Section B	Payment details	
Period	01/07/20Y1 to 30/06/20Y2	
Payee TFN	345678912	
Total tax withheld	752 *seven hundred and fifty-two dollars*	
Gross payments	3010	
Allowances	Tool	100
	Travel	210
Union dues	Electrical Trades Union	35

Section C	Payer details
Payer's ABN	1234 12345
Payer's name	Big Daddy Electrical Contractors

Note that the layout of the payslip matches the information required on the payment summary. The closer the payslip matches the requirements of the payment summary, the easier it is for you to complete the payment summary.

Revision exercise for day 6

Big Daddy is replacing Alex with:

- Tom Smith—hourly rate $45

- Richard Little—hourly rate $25.

Both new employees receive a tool allowance of $50 per week and travel at $0.60 per kilometre. They pay $35 per pay to the Electrical Trades Union.

- Fortnight ending 1/06/11—Tom worked 80 hours and claimed 345k mileage. Richard worked 80 hours plus 8 hours overtime at time and one half and claimed 456k mileage.

- Fortnight ending 14/06/11—Tom worked 80 hours and claimed 245k mileage and Richard worked 80 hours and claimed 214k mileage.

- Fortnight ending 28/06/11—Tom worked 80 hours plus 8 hours overtime at time and one half and claimed 290k mileage and Richard worked 80 hours and claimed 314k mileage.

1 Complete a payslip for each of the employees for each period (ignore the leave balances in this example). Use MySuper as the super fund of choice.

2 Complete a payment summary as at 30/6/11 for each employee.

Day 7

Other issues in payroll

Key terms and concepts

▶ *Unused leave entitlements:* annual and long service leave not used by the employee.

▶ *Annual leave:* an entitlement of full-time and part-time employees to paid leave (usually 20 paid days) each year.

▶ *Long service leave:* leave accrued over a long period, usually three months over 15 years, that is paid out (pro rata) on termination after 10 years.

▶ *Employment termination payment:* amount paid on termination of employment that is not included in the normal last pay and is concessionally taxed, such as a 'golden handshake' (lump sum paid on termination).

▶ *Drawings:* an amount withdrawn from the business by the owner in cash or goods in anticipation of profits.

▶ *Salary:* fixed annual amount paid to professional and executive staff irrespective of the actual hours worked.

▶ *Wages:* an amount paid to an employee based on an hourly rate.

▶ *Casual:* an employee paid by the hour on a needs basis who may be entitled to overtime if they work more than 38 hours during the week.

▶ *Contractor:* a service provider who works under contract to perform a specific function.

▶ *Tax offsets:* concessional amounts that can be claimed by the taxpayer to offset the normal amount of tax payable.

▶ *Holiday leave loading:* 17.5 per cent of normal pay, paid at the time the employee takes their annual leave. Available only to certain employees working under an award that includes this payment.

▶ *Medicare levy:* 1.5 per cent included in the tax withheld from salary and wages to pay for the public health system.

▶ *Fringe benefits tax (FBT):* a tax paid by the employer on benefits provided for the private use of an employee or associate of an employee, such as gym memberships or school fees.

▶ *FBT exemption:* amounts that can be applied for the private use of an employee that do not attract the FBT.

▶ *Private use:* a use of business monies or assets that are not for the direct benefit of the business, but are for the benefit of the employee.

▶ *FBT gross-up factor:* a factor applied to an employee's benefits to take into account that tax that would normally be paid by the employee on that income.

Paying the boss—drawings versus salary

It is normal for a business owner to take an amount of cash or goods out of the business on a regular basis. This drawing is more than likely referred to as the owner's wages.

However, if you run your own small business, either as a sole proprietor (such as a lawnmowing contractor) or in a partnership, then you cannot 'legally' pay yourself a salary or wage. Any monies (or goods) that you take out of the business are considered a drawing in anticipation of profits (a reduction in equity) and not a salary or wage expense. No taxes are withheld from the owner's drawings. The owner's income tax liability is based on the profits of the business.

On the other hand, if you are the owner of a company (a director in the legal sense), your drawings are classed as a salary or wage and you will need to be 'employed'; that is, abide by the same legal and tax requirements as any other employee. In the case of a company, the entity pays company tax and the owner pays income tax on their salary (drawings) and includes the company dividends and franking credits in their annual tax returns.

Employee or contractor?

The first question we must ask ourselves is 'Who exactly are our employees?'

Businesses often employ staff who are employees under the common law definition of master and servant, but they can also employ staff under contractual arrangements. If these staff are employed through an agency with whom you have an ongoing relationship—that is, the agency bills you for the employees' time and you settle the account with the agency—then the employee is a contractor and therefore outside the PAYG system (as far as your business is concerned). However, if contractors are employed directly by the business, at what point does a contract employee become a wages employee?

According to the ATO, a worker is an employee if they:

▶ are paid for time worked

▶ receive paid leave (for example, sick, annual or recreation, or long service leave)

- ▶ are not responsible for providing the materials or equipment required to do their job
- ▶ must perform the duties of their position
- ▶ agree to provide their personal services
- ▶ work hours set by an agreement or award
- ▶ are recognised as part and parcel of the payer's business
- ▶ take no commercial risks and cannot make a profit or loss from the work performed.

An independent contractor is an entity (such as an individual, partnership, trust or company) who agrees to produce a designated result for an agreed price. The ATO states that, in most cases, an independent contractor:

- ▶ is paid for results achieved
- ▶ provides all or most of the necessary materials and equipment to complete the work
- ▶ is free to delegate work to other entities
- ▶ has freedom in the way the work is done
- ▶ provides services to the general public and other businesses
- ▶ is free to accept or refuse work
- ▶ is in a position to make a profit or loss.

An employee is paid a wage and has tax and other deductions taken from their pay, whereas a contractor provides you with an invoice that includes a bill for their services and GST where applicable. You pay this invoice as you would any other expense.

Contractors are not usually covered by your workers' compensation and therefore you should ensure that all workers have their own workers' compensation insurance coverage.

Tax offsets

Item 10 on your employee's tax file number (employee) declaration asks if the employee wants to claim zone, overseas forces, dependant spouse or special tax offsets. What are these?

Tax offsets can be claimed by a taxpayer in certain circumstances through their annual tax return. Examples include a zone allowance where the employee works in a remote location, or a spouse rebate where the employee's spouse's income is less than a prescribed amount. These amounts are claimed by the employee through a withholding declaration form. The amount claimed on this form is a matter between the employee and the Tax Office. If you receive the form then you put the payday amount into the TWC calculator as shown in figure 7.1 (refer to day 6 for more about the TWC calculator).

Figure 7.1: add the payday amount to the TWC calculator

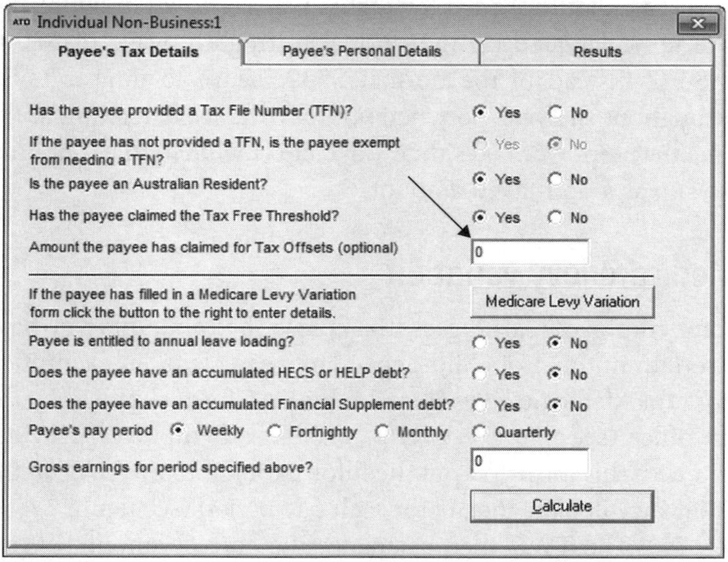

167

The withholding declaration form is also used to vary any information originally provided on the tax file number (employee) declaration form and also is used where the employee wishes to vary the amount of tax you withhold from their wages.

Holiday leave loading

Certain industrial award conditions, such as the award for cleaners, require an employer to pay the employee 17.5 per cent of their normal wages as a loading when the employee takes annual leave. For example, if an employee's normal pay is $2000 per fortnight and they go on leave for the fortnight, you are required to pay them an additional $350 in leave loading. The main problem with leave loading is that it is taxed progressively throughout the year and not at the time of payment.

If your employee is entitled to a leave loading indicate it on the TWC calculator for each fortnight's pay as shown in figure 7.2. The tax calculated on the normal fortnightly wage of $2000 is $542 instead of the normal $539. Leave loading is taxed throughout the year, so when you pay the leave loading at the time the employee takes their leave, it is included in the holiday payslip as a non-taxed amount.

Medicare levy variation

Some employees earning less than prescribed amounts who have a certain number of child dependants can claim an exemption from the Medicare levy. They do this on a form supplied by the tax office (see figure 7.3 on p. 170). If an employee provides you with this form you put the information into the TWC at the time you calculate the tax for each pay period (see figure 7.4 on p. 171). The TWC then calculates the correct amount of tax, including the reduced Medicare levy, for that employee.

Figure 7.2: if your employee is entitled to leave loading, include it on the TWC calculator

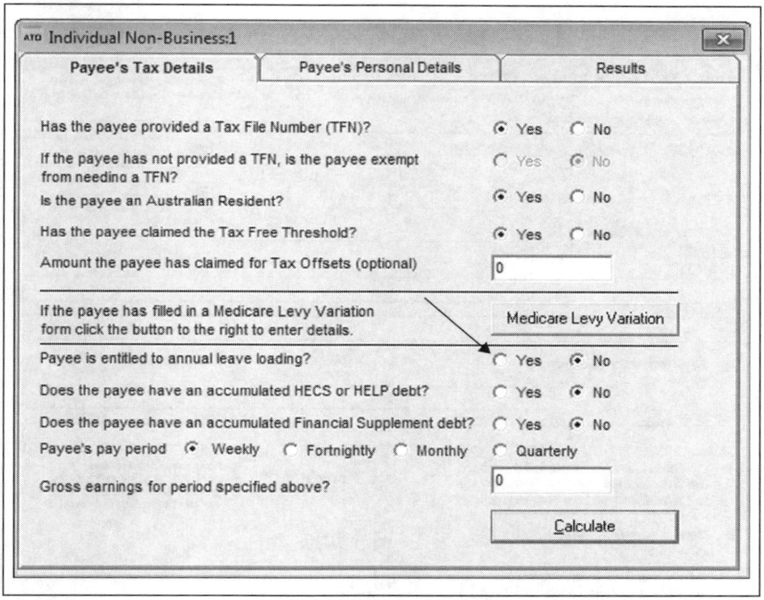

Termination of employment

This discussion of employment termination is limited to the normal 'brown bag' termination where an employee leaves of their own accord. I do not discuss redundancy, retirement or forced resignation. It is also assumed that your employee has been with your firm for less than 15 years.

When an employee terminates their employment, they are paid out any leave balance owing. Leave balances, including annual leave and any long service leave (including pro rata payments) are included in an employee's gross income and taxed accordingly. There are no longer any special provisions for these types of payments.

Figure 7.3: Medicare levy variation declaration form

Australian Government
Australian Taxation Office **Medicare levy variation declaration form**

■ Refer to the Instructions to help you complete this declaration.
■ Print neatly in BLOCK LETTERS and use a black or dark blue pen.
■ Print *X* in the appropriate boxes.

● The information in the completed *Medicare levy variation declaration* form must be treated in confidence.

Section A: Payee's declaration

● To be completed by payee.

1 What is your tax file number (TFN)?

● See 'Privacy of information' on the inside front cover of the Instructions.

2 What is your name?
Title: Mr ☐ Mrs ☐ Miss ☐ Ms ☐ Other ☐
Family name

Given names

3 What is your home address?
Street address

Suburb/town | State/Territory | Postcode

4 Do you want your payer to increase the amounts withheld from you by 1% to cover the Medicare levy surcharge? No ☐ Go to question 5. Yes ☐ If you want to make other variations using this form, go to question 5. Otherwise, sign and date the declaration and give it to your payer.

5 Do you qualify for a Medicare levy exemption? No ☐ Go to question 8. Yes ☐

6 Do you want to claim a full exemption from the Medicare levy? No ☐ Yes ☐ Go to question 9.

7 Do you want to claim a half levy exemption from the Medicare levy? No ☐ Yes ☐ Go to question 9.

8 Do you want to claim a Medicare levy reduction? No ☐ Yes ☐

9 Do you have a spouse? No ☐ Yes ☐ ● See the Glossary on page 5 for a definition of spouse.

10 Is the combined weekly income of you and your spouse, or your income as a sole parent, less than the relevant amount in table A on page 1? No ☐ Yes ☐

11a Do you have an accumulated Higher Education Loan Program (HELP) debt? No ☐ Yes ☐ If you also answered 'YES' at question 10, you are exempt from having additional PAYG amounts for HELP withheld from payments to you.

11b Do you have an accumulated Financial Supplement debt? No ☐ Yes ☐ If you also answered 'YES' at question 10, you are exempt from having additional PAYG amounts for Financial Supplement debts withheld from payments to you.

12 Do you have dependent children? No ☐ Sign and date the declaration. Yes ☐ How many? ☐

● See the Glossary on page 5 for a definition of dependent children.

NAT 0929-07.2010 **IN-CONFIDENCE – when completed**

Figure 7.4: if an employee claims an exemption from the Medicare levy, add the information to the TWC calculator

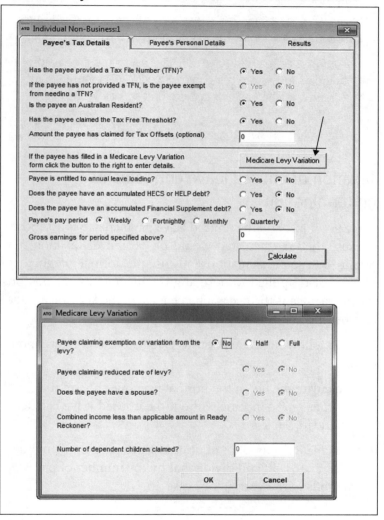

Example 1 (refer to Alex in day 6)

The payday of 19/07/20Y1 was Alex's last day with the firm. How would this modify the payslip and the payment summary?

Her annual leave entitlement of 70.9 hours must be paid out and added to her gross income. Her sick leave entitlement is foregone and she has no accrued long service leave:

$$70.9 \times \$35.00 = \$2481.50$$

Taxation of unused leave entitlements on termination

You cannot just add the unused leave payments to gross income because the tax calculated would be excessive. Taxation rules require that such calculations only use the normal marginal rate of tax that is applied to normal gross income tax calculations. 'Marginal' means the tax as a percentage of the last dollar added to gross income.

Use the following calculation to calculate the correct amount of tax:

1   Calculate the tax in the normal way but only on the 'normal' gross income without the unused leave balances included. This is $702.

2   Calculate the amount of unused leave payments, in our case $2481.50 and divide that by the number of pay periods in the year, in our case 26:

$$\$2481.50/26 = \$95.44$$

3   To the normal gross income add the 1/26th of the leave payment:

$$3010.00 + 95.44 = \$3105.44$$

4   Calculate the tax on this figure using the TWC calculator. This comes to $734.

5   Work out the difference between the two tax amounts:

$$\$734 - \$702 = \$32$$

Multiply that difference by 26:

$$\$32 \times 26 = \$832.$$

The tax payable on the unused leave balance paid on termination of employment is $832.

Total tax payable is:

$$\$702 + \$832 = \$1534.$$

Compare $1532 with $1652, which is the amount we calculated on normal gross income plus the leave balance amount.

The termination payslip is shown in figure 7.5 (overleaf).

Employment termination payments

An employment (formerly eligible) **termination payment** (ETP), which is paid when employment is terminated, is the payment of certain amounts that are concessionally taxed, depending on the type and age of the payment. Significant changes were made in the taxation of ETPs in July 2007 although some transitional changes apply until June 2012:

▶   ETPs can no longer be rolled over into superannuation (except transitional arrangements)

▶   ETPs need to be made within 12 months of termination to qualify for reduced tax benefits (excluding genuine redundancy payments)

▶   a cap or limit applies for amounts to qualify for the lower tax benefit.

Figure 7.5: termination payslip

Big Daddy Electrical Contractors
22 Fairfield Crescent, Nowhere NSW 2789
ABN 1234 12345

Pay date	19/07/20Y1	*Termination pay*
Employee	Ms Alex Hanson	
Pay period	01/07/20Y1 to 14/07/20Y1	

Wages

Wages	9 days at 8 hours at $35.00	2520.00
Overtime	4 hours at 1.5	210.00
Sick leave 8 hours		280.00
Normal pay for this period		**3010.00**
Annual leave	70.9 hours @ $35.00	2481.50
		5491.50

Allowances

Tool allowance	100.00
Travel 230k at $0.60	210.00
Gross pay	**5801.50**

Deductions

Income tax on normal pay	702.00
Income tax payable on leave balances	832.00
Additional tax	50.00
Union dues (Electrical Trades Union)	35.00
Medibank Private	55.00
Amount paid (ANZ ***345)	**4127.50**

Superannuation
9% employer's contribution of $252.00 paid into ETU Superannuation

Payments included in ETPs include:

▶ payment in lieu of notice

▶ payout of rostered days off entitlement

▶ a gratuity, golden handshake or compensation for loss of employment

▶ payments resulting in termination because of ill health, invalidity or personal injury

▶ payments for wrongful dismissal

▶ payments for genuine redundancy or early retirement in excess of tax-free limit.

Amounts that accumulated for pre-1983 employment or as a consequence of invalidity may be tax free in some circumstances. The transitional arrangements that apply to the taxation of ETPs apply only to amounts paid under a contract that was in force as at 9 May 2006. Special arrangements apply to death benefits paid as an ETP.

A detailed discussion of these provisions is beyond the 'brown bag' scope of this text. Please refer to the Tax Office publication on employment termination payments for further information in these cases.

The taxation of ETPs

How ETPs are taxed depends on the ETP cap. The ETP cap amount for the 2008–09 financial year was $145 000. The ETP cap is indexed in line with the average weekly ordinary time earnings (AWOTE) in increments of $5000 (rounded down).

▶ If the total amount of the payment (even if paid in a number of instalments over different tax years) exceeds the cap then the excess is taxed at 46.5 per cent.

▶ If the total payments do not exceed the cap amount and the employee is less than 55 years of age on the last day of the income year, a flat tax rate of 31.5 per cent applies.

▶ If the total payments do not exceed the cap amount and the employee is more than 55 years of age, then a flat tax rate of 16.5 per cent applies.

If you need to make an ETP payment, report it to the Tax Office on a PAYG payment summary—employment termination payment form (NAT 70868) (see figure 7.6).

Keeping records

Your obligations to employees and other workers come from a variety of sources—federal, state and territory laws, industrial awards and agreements, tribunal decisions and contracts of employment (whether they are written or verbal).

According to business.gov.au, some of your obligations as an employer include:

▶ paying correct wages

▶ reimbursing your employees for work-related expenses

▶ ensuring a safe working environment

▶ not acting in a way that may seriously damage an employee's reputation or cause mental distress or humiliation

▶ not acting in a way that damages the trust and confidence necessary for an employment relationship

▶ not providing a false or misleading reference

▶ forwarding PAYE tax instalments to the Tax Office

▶ making appropriate payment under the superannuation guarantee legislation.

The records that you keep go in part to satisfying these requirements.

Create a separate file for each employee. The first document is usually the person's application for the position, records kept of the interview, letters sent and acceptances received, and any

Figure 7.6: PAYG payment summary—employment termination payment form

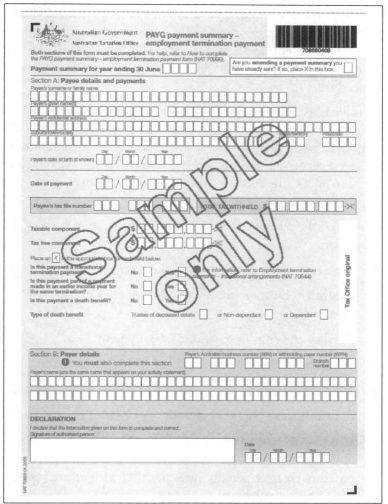

employment contracts entered into. The qualifications required by the person to perform the job should also be included; for example, proof of trade qualifications and any necessary trade certification. Once employed, the first document to be added to the employee file should be the TFN declaration, as well as proof that the employee has undertaken an indoctrination procedure.

This file is usually kept as a master file, with pay records for each employee kept in separate pay files on a year-by-year basis. All employee records must be kept and be accessible for a minimum of seven years, and are private and confidential. Generally, no-one can access the records other than the employee, employer and relevant payroll staff.

Your records, when viewed as a whole, must at least show the following:

► the name of the employer and the name of the employee

► Australian business number (ABN) (if any) of the employer

► the date the employee started employment

► whether the employee is full time or part time

► whether the employee is permanent, temporary or casual

► the employee's pay rate, including gross and net amounts paid and any deductions from the gross amount

► any loadings, monetary allowances, bonuses, incentive-based payments, penalty rates or other entitlements paid that can be singled out

► whether a penalty rate or loading must be paid for overtime hours actually worked, the number of hours of overtime worked, or when the employee started and finished working overtime

▶ hours worked if the employee works casual or irregular part-time hours and is guaranteed a pay rate set by reference to a period of time worked

▶ a copy of the written agreement if you and your employee have agreed to average the employee's work hours

▶ whether you and your employee have agreed to an individual flexibility arrangement, a copy of that agreement and, if the agreement is terminated, a copy of the termination

▶ leave information for all types of leave, including:

    ¤ leave taken

    ¤ leave balance

    ¤ a copy of any agreement to cash out accrued leave, the rate of payment for the leave and when the payment was made

▶ for employees paid superannuation (excluding payments to a defined benefit fund), the:

    ¤ amount paid

    ¤ pay period

    ¤ date(s) paid

    ¤ name of super fund

    ¤ reason you paid super into the fund (for example, a record of the employee's super fund choice and the date that choice was made)

▶ if the employment is terminated:

    ¤ who terminated the employment

    ¤ how the termination took place — by consent, notice, summarily or in some other way (include details).

Payroll fraud

Some employees will be tempted to steal from their employer. Fraud in general is dealt with in day 5. Here we are specifically dealing with payroll fraud.

There is a simple rule that will help you prevent employees stealing from you and that rule is to be vigilant. If you do not double-check, or have checks and balances in place, then you will be targeted. A disgruntled employee, an employee under financial strain or an employee with a gambling or drug habit are all potential instigators of fraud. No-one is immune. Payroll fraud can happen at any time and in a variety of ways. We will now deal with two of the most common types of payroll fraud: phantom employees and payroll manipulation.

Phantom employees

A phantom employee is an employee who exists only on paper within your payroll system, not in reality. The head count of your employees is one of the most basic auditing techniques, used both by your own internal or external audit staff and also by the Tax Office, union and Work Cover payroll auditors.

Phantom employees can be created in a variety of ways. The most common is where a line manager has the ability to hire staff and there are no counterchecks on this. For example, a warehouse manager may be able to employ casual staff and needs only to send through the TFN declaration and employee details as proof of employment for payroll purposes. In this situation, it is too easy for the manager to submit fake details of a short-term casual employee, with the manager's own bank account as details for payment.

Another common method in the smaller business is for the payroll officer to create fake records and substitute their own bank account details for payment.

However, the most common method of creating a phantom employee is where a genuine employee leaves your employ but the line manager does not notify payroll of the termination. Instead of submitting a termination notice the manager puts through a change of details form and redirects the phantom employee's pay into their own account.

How do you prevent phantom employees? The first step is to identify managers who can employ staff and ensure that the payroll clerk is not one of them. Next, instigate an office process that requires all new employees, with no exceptions, to be interviewed by a human resource management or payroll staff member to ensure that the TFN declaration is correctly completed and that the employee's details are correctly entered into the system. Any changes to the employee's details, especially change of bank details, should be presented to the payroll officer by the employee themselves. Managers will attempt to get around this requirement and, if they do, they should be brought back into line in the sternest way.

In smaller firms, you should instigate a 'meet and greet' policy for all new employees. This handshake policy ensures all new employees actually exist. If a line manager tries to get around this policy they must be quickly brought back into line.

Records manipulation

This example shows how records manipulation can occur.

You employ a payroll clerk, Alice, for $25 per hour for a 35-hour week. She performs her job very well and you start to trust her to handle the payroll process. Alice cannot meet her mortgage payments, however, and is about to lose her house. All she needs is an extra $70 per week.

Alice's solution is to change her payroll records to pay herself $28 per hour. This results in an extra $105 per week which after tax gives her more than the $70 she needs. Problem solved!

The big question is how would you pick up changes to the payroll records such as paying overtime that was never done or allowances that are not due? You must ensure that on each payday all of your payroll records are reviewed for changes in base rates and compared with source documents such as timesheets for any additional items. Often such verification procedures, or internal controls, can be built into normal business processes.

The basic tenet of a good internal control system is that every process in the business is cross-checked by an independent person. Internal controls are discussed further in day 5.

An overview of fringe benefits tax

To really understand fringe benefits tax (FBT) you must first understand the underlying history of this tax. Before 1970 it was unusual for an employee to be paid in any form other than cash. During the 1970s a trend started to develop where mainly executive employees were provided with a motor vehicle as part of their overall remuneration. These vehicles were usually used primarily, but not solely, for work purposes.

However, by the 1980s the concept of salary packaging (a base salary with benefits such as a company car that is also available for private use) had grown to the extent that it was becoming popular for an employee's private expenses such as their mortgage and children's school fees to be paid by their employer as part of the total remuneration package. Because these items were paid outside of the salary system they were effectively tax free. Fringe benefits tax legislation was introduced in 1986 to tax these private expenses.

Fringe benefits tax is paid by the employer on all fringe benefits paid on behalf of their employees (or associates of employees) at the top marginal individual rate of 48.5 per cent. If an item has both a private and business use, only the private portion is subject to FBT.

The FBT tax year is from 1 April to 31 March so that it does not coincide with the 30 June income tax year. The benefit supplied and the FBT paid are tax deductions to the employer, in the same manner as wages and salaries, so the benefit provided to the employee has to also be adjusted for any income tax that would normally be payable by the employee. This gross-up factor (type 1) is based upon the top marginal income tax rate. Appendix A explains FBT gross-up factors.

In 2000 Australia introduced the GST and this has caused some problems in calculating FBT payable. Most of the benefits provided by an employer are subject to GST and the employer is entitled to a GST credit for this expenditure, so the FBT calculation has to 'claw back' this GST credit. It does this through an adjusted gross-up factor called a type 2 factor.

The easiest way for an employer to avoid FBT is to:

▶ pay employees a wage that does not include any private use of company assets

▶ pay employees an allowance to cover the business use of private assets that they own, such as their home telephone

▶ ensure that employees (including company business owners) reimburse the firm for the private use of business assets. This is known as the contributory method.

FBT exemptions

Not all items provided by an employer to an employee that include a private portion are subject to FBT. For example, the incidental use of business phones or computers to make private phone calls or to send private emails is not subject to FBT under the 'reasonable use' provisions. Any benefit that you provide to an employee for which the employee would normally be entitled to an income tax deduction, such as union or professional association fees, is not subject to FBT under the 'otherwise deductible' rule. The payment of superannuation into a complying superannuation fund, including any salary sacrifice amounts, is specifically exempt from the FBT rules.

In addition to these general exemptions, there are also specific work-related exemptions. You can provide an employee with one of each of the items listed below per FBT year (excluding a replacement for damaged, lost or stolen items) provided that the item supplied was mainly intended to be used for work-related purposes; that is, at the time the item was supplied its intended use was mainly work related:

► portable electronic devices (one of each) such as mobile phone, calculator, PDA, laptop, portable printer and GPS system

► computer software for the portable devices listed above or for the employee's home computer that they use for work-related matters

► protective clothing

► briefcase

► tool(s) of trade (one of each item used primarily for work-related purposes, not including replacements).

If an employer pays any amount on behalf of an employee, or provides an employee with the use of a business asset and

1   that payment or provision has a private use component, *and*

2   the item or payment is not covered by either the general or specific exemption listed above,

the private use portion of that benefit is subject to FBT.

The provision of assets or payment of expenses, referred to as a fringe benefit, is usually paid to employees, but also includes the provision of a benefit to the business owners or the 'associates' of employees or owners (that is, their family members). All private use of business assets is handled under FBT rules irrespective of the business structure.

Accounting for employee's private use

Accounting for employees' private use can be done in one of two ways.

Firstly, you can provide the employee with an allowance that is included in their salary; for example, a home phone allowance. The allowance can either be a fixed amount or in the form of a reimbursement of expenses. Either way the allowance is taxed as a component of the employee's salary. It is up to the employee to claim the business use as a deduction against the allowance income in their tax return and to justify the expenditure. In many ways, from an employer's viewpoint this is the easiest method, but claiming GST credits on business use of employee assets may be a problem.

If you pay a fixed allowance each period, the GST credits could be lost; however, this is usually an insignificant amount. If the amount of the GST credit is substantial, you should ask the employee to make a claim on you (a reimbursement) for their business expenses, including copies of the original tax invoices. You can then reimburse them through their salary and claim the GST credits accordingly. The easiest way to handle sales representative motor vehicle expenses, for example, is to pay a fixed allowance to cover the purchase cost (business percentage of loan repayments) of the vehicle and then ask the employee to claim petrol and other expenses by reimbursement.

Secondly, you can pay the phone account or other expense and claim the amount as a tax deduction against the business. You can then either ask the employee to reimburse the business for the private portion of the expense (such as the phone account), either by actual payment (income to the business or offset against the expense) or by deducting the private use amount from the employee's *after-tax* salary. Business use of home phones can only apply to phone calls and those calls must be justified as business related by written evidence, such as the phone bill identifying the call as a business or through a diary. The home phone line rental should never be classed as a business expense.

If you use this second method, you must write back the private use proportion of the GST credit claimed on payment of the account when the private use payment is made. This is more complex than the reimbursement method and for that reason the first method is preferable.

If you provide the employee with a business asset which they also use for private purposes, such as a motor vehicle or a home computer, then you must also account for the private use proportion by either of the methods above. If you do not seek reimbursement (an employee contribution in FBT terms) of the private use proportion of the expenses paid or assets used, *that amount will be subject to FBT.*

Categories of private use

The fringe benefits rules contain a number of categories of expenses, each with its own calculations used to determine the private use proportion. The last category is residual benefits into which everything else falls. The main benefits that affect a small business are:

▶ expense payments

▶ property

▶ car parking (does not apply to onsite parking for small business)

▶ meal entertainment.

The main category not included in this list is motor vehicles, which are discussed on day 2 as part of business assets accounting.

Expense fringe benefit is the value of any expenses the employer pays on behalf of the employee, such as school fees or club membership, or for which the employer reimburses the employee, other than by means of a taxable allowance as part of the salary package.

Property fringe benefit is where the employer buys an asset, such as a computer, for an employee and gives that computer to the employee (ownership passes to the employee) for their own personal use. This is distinct from the employer providing the employee with *access* to, or use of, a PC which is normally work related only. The value of the fringe benefit is the value of the property provided less any employee contribution. The employee can then claim a deduction against their income for the business use of the asset.

Car parking fringe benefit applies only to small businesses (less than $10m turnover) where it is provided at a commercial parking station. Incidental parking costs (less than $100 per year) are exempt, as is work-related parking, for example visiting clients.

Meal entertainment fringe benefit is where you, or your employee, take a client out for a meal. Under income tax rules the provision of meals for clients is not an allowable deduction. However, if you wish to use the FBT provisions you can deduct 50 per cent of the meal value and that 50 per cent is subject to FBT. An employer can spend $50 on each employee under this category, such as for a Christmas lunch, without incurring a fringe benefit and being allowed a tax deduction for the expense.

Other forms of FBT include:

▶ loans granted

▶ debt waiver

▶ housing

▶ living-away-from-home allowance

▶ board.

The tax payable on the private portion of the benefit is determined differently for each of these benefits. For example, the tax payable on a loan given to an employee depends upon the interest rate charged to the employee.

Private use by company owners

The simple rule for purchases by owners for their own private use out of business funds is that such purchases are debited to the drawings account and repaid in the form of a salary conversion. You do not claim the GST credit on private use purchases.

Part business and part private purchases are best handled by apportioning the GST and crediting the drawings account with the balance. An item costing $110, of which 70 per cent was for business use, could be apportioned $70 to the expense account, $7 GST credit and $33 to the owner's drawings account. This is the same method used for individuals and partnerships, but for companies the drawings account must subsequently be converted into salary.

The main problem occurs with depreciating assets. If they are 100 per cent private use, then you treat them as above. If they are for part business and part private use then the strict tax treatment is to claim the GST credit in full and debit the asset to a depreciation account, then claim the depreciation in full (no private portion deduction). You then must pay FBT on the market value of the private use proportion. However, the Tax Office will not advise you on how to determine the market value of this use. Your accountant is the best person to turn to in these circumstances.

The alternative method of dealing with depreciable assets used partly for private use is to use the apportionment approach. On purchase you only claim the GST credit on the business portion of the expense and you only claim depreciation on the business portion of the asset.

An alternative treatment is available to owners of companies. In these cases the owners, as 'employees' of the business, may elect to pay for their private use through the FBT rules; that is, to lodge an FBT return and pay tax on private use at the top marginal rate, currently 45 per cent plus the Medicare levy.

However, in the case where owners could use FBT, it is better to adopt the contributory method rather than pay the FBT. Using this method you account for your private use by 'paying back' the private portion through the drawings account. Where there is no private use, there is no fringe benefit. The contributory method can also be used for employees' private use, although an allowance method, making the payment part of the employee's wages, is recommended as this is simpler from a business accounting perspective.

If you decide to pay FBT rather than use the contributory method, your private use is taxed as a tax inclusive fringe benefit. In this case your expense is 100 per cent income tax deductible and your GST 100 per cent creditable. The private use tax consequences are incorporated into the FBT calculations.

Accounting for FBT

If you wish to use fringe benefits to account for private use benefits, create three new account expense codes:

FBT type 1—GST paid (including an unregistered entity)

FBT type 2—no GST

FBT expense.

The accounting methodology is to allocate to FBT type 1 the amount of private use that includes a GST credit (if you are registered for the GST). The same applies for type 2, but for expenses that do not include a GST credit (or all expenditure if you are not registered for the GST). These accounts help you reconcile your FBT paid on the BAS and the FBT return. The FBT expense account holds the FBT tax paid; it is a deduction for income tax purposes. For example:

Electricity	$20	*business use proportion*
FBT type 1	$80	*private use excluding GST*
GST account	$10	*full GST credit*
Bank	$110	*the actual amount paid*

When making the payment above, ensure that the detail states that it is an electricity payment. This will make reconciliation of the FBT type accounts easier.

If you elect to use FBT for private expenses you need to register for fringe benefits tax. You can do this at the time you apply for your ABN or at any time after this. You need to fill in an FBT return by 28 April each year for the year 1 April to 31 March (not the tax year).

Filling in the FBT return is not hard. Pages 1 and 2 are essentially just your name and address. Page 3 is the calculations. A sample of a fringe benefits form is available from my website <www.tpabusiness.com.au>.

The amount of FBT you pay is an allowable tax deduction (FBT expense account). This is because it is akin to wages and salaries, and in the same category as PAYG deductions. However, the purchases used for private purposes also qualify for GST credits in full, without any private use deduction. To allow for both of these treatments your private use proportion must be grossed up before you apply the tax rate to the gross amount.

First, add together (aggregate) all private use amounts that contain a GST credit. These are known as type 1 amounts (FBT type 1 account). Next, add together all private use amounts that do not contain a GST credit (FBT type 2 account). These are amounts for which you do not claim the credit because you are not registered for the GST or amounts from an invoice that did not contain a GST amount. These are known as type 2 amounts.

At the appropriate item in the FBT return enter the aggregate amount for type 1 and then type 2, then multiply the type 1 amounts by 2.0647 and the type 2 amounts by 1.8692. Enter and add together the amounts to get the gross figure to which you apply the FBT tax rate of 46.5 per cent. This is the amount you pay! If you have been paying your FBT as part of your quarterly BAS statement then deduct your total payments for the year (1 April to 31 March) from the amount payable and this is the amount either payable or subject to a refund.

You also need to fill in the statistical portion that breaks up your FBT amounts into FBT categories. If you are using the account codes method mentioned earlier (FBT type 1 account and so on), note the reason for each payment so that you can correctly analyse the FBT type accounts and place the amounts into the appropriate category.

A final note on FBT payments

Fringe benefits tax payments are deductible expenses to the business, but under the simplified tax system, cash accounting entities can only deduct the tax when they actually pay it. Like other taxes, you pay your FBT as a forward estimate on your BAS or IAS (instalment activity statement) if you are not registered for the GST. When you lodge your annual FBT return the Tax Office will estimate your liability for FBT for the next year and include that estimate on your BAS if you paid more than $3000 of FBT this year. You have to pay this estimate even if your current year FBT liability is going to be less than $3000. You will get a refund of the excess when you lodge your annual return. If your current year FBT is more than the estimate, you pay the estimate on your BAS and the difference with your annual return.

Where the total value of all benefits provided to any employee (including any of their associates) is more than $2000 for the FBT year (ending 31 March), the employee's annual payment summary (as at 30 June) must contain the amount as a reportable fringe benefit. The amount reported on the payment summary is the grossed-up amount (by the lower factor of 1.8692) and not just the base value. This will not affect the employee's income tax liability, but it could affect any payments based upon the employee's gross salary, for example child support payments.

Revision exercise for day 7

Tom is paid $45 per hour for an 80 hour fortnight. His annual leave entitlement on resignation was 20.5 hours. How much tax would he pay on this entitlement?

Appendix A

FBT gross-up factors explained

When working out the value of a benefit, the benefit is grossed up by a factor of either 1.8692 or 2.0647. Why?

Type 2 — no GST implications

The FBT rate is set at the top marginal tax rate. For the FBT tax year that ended on 31 March 2011 the rate was 46.5 per cent (45 per cent plus 1.5 per cent Medicare levy). This tax is not paid on the value of the benefit, however, but on the grossed-up value.

Fringe benefits tax is based upon the assumption that the employee who is getting the benefit is being taxed at the top marginal rate, whether this is the case or not. Therefore, as the FBT is a substitute for the tax that the employee would normally pay on the benefit, the FBT liability is worked out in the following way.

Let's assume that the benefit paid was $1000 for a golf club membership. What gross salary would the employee have to be paid in order to pay this membership out of their after-tax income?

What amount less tax at 46.5%   = $1000

= 1000 ÷ (100 − 46.5%)
= $1869.20

$1869.20 × 46.5%   = $869.20 tax paid

$1869.20 − $869.20   = $1000 after-tax income
                          to pay the membership

Therefore the true value of the membership to the employee is $1869.20. This is also the amount you declare on the employee's income statement as a reportable fringe benefit.

Type 1—adding GST into the mix

Let us assume that the employer was registered for the GST. The actual payment would have been $1000 for the membership plus $100 that was claimed as a GST credit. Therefore, in order to determine the true value of the benefit we must add the GST credit into the mix. Let us assume that the amount paid was $1100, which was made up of the $1000 benefit plus $100 GST credit. What would our employee need to be paid in order to cover this cost?

What amount less tax at 46.5%   = $1000 + a GST credit
                          of $100

= 1100 ÷ (100 − 46.5%)
= $2056.07

$2056.07 × 46.5%   = $956.07 tax paid

$2056.07 − 956.07   = $1100 after-tax income
                          to pay the membership

Therefore the true value of the GST inclusive membership to the employee is $2056.07. However, you do not use this for reportable fringe benefits purposes, but instead use the lower type 2 factor of 1.8692.

FBT gross-up rates

The FBT gross-up rates for 2011 are:

▶ *Type 1*: where the employer is registered for the GST and there is a GST credit in the benefit provided, the value of the benefit (after accounting for the GST component) is grossed up by a factor of 2.0647

▶ *Type 2*: where no GST credit is involved in the benefit (including where the employer is not registered for the GST), the gross-up figure to use is 1.8692.

Appendix B
Useful resources

Author's website

On my website <www.tpabusiness.com.au>, under 'Learn Small Business Accounting in 7 Days', you will find resources for the student and lecturer. These resources include:

▶ an example of a balance sheet and income statement layout

▶ the conceptual framework

▶ examples of effective life (taken from the tax office ruling)

▶ an example of a fringe benefits return

▶ many worked examples in Excel.

Australian Taxation Office fact sheets

The following fact sheets are available from the ATO website <www.ato.gov.au>. Just type the relevant 'NAT' number indicated into the search box to go straight to the publication you wish to access. Some of these fact sheets can be downloaded as PDF files and others can only be read onscreen or printed for your reference:

▶ *Effective life of depreciating assets* (TR 2010/2)

▶ *Employment termination payments—when an employee leaves* (NAT 71043)

▶ *Guide to depreciating assets* (NAT 1996)

▶ *How to complete the PAYG payment summary* (NAT 3388)

▶ *Medicare levy variation declaration (instructions)* (NAT 0929)

▶ *Super—what employers need to know* (NAT 71038)

▶ *Withholding declaration (variation form and instructions)* (NAT 3093).

In addition, the following guides are available from the ATO's website <www.ato.gov.au> (go to the business tab):

▶ Fringe benefits tax—a guide for employers

▶ Fringe benefits tax for small business

▶ Fringe benefits tax—what you need to know.

Appendix C
Revision exercise solutions

The theory questions for each day are available from my website at <www.tpabusiness.com.au>.

Day 2: Assets, depreciation and registers

Initial purchase:

16/3/2011	Lathe	2700	
	GST	270	
	Private use	1980	
	Cash at bank		4950

Being: the initial purchase of the wood-working lathe

Wood-working lathe   **1510**

Date	Particulars	Folio	Debit	Credit	Balance
16/03/2011	Cash	GJ_N	2700.00		2700.00

Effective life from TR 2010: 13.33 years.

Lathes

Computer controlled	10.00
Engineering works (machinery installed)	20.00
Wood-working plant	13.33

Depreciation schedule:

Asset			Wood-working lathe	
Cost			$2700.00	
Effective life			13.33 years	
Depreciation rate			11.25%	
Date	Opening value	Second element cost	Depreciation	Closing value
16/03/2011				2700.00
30/06/2011	2700.00		88.23	2611.77
30/06/2012	2611.77		293.90	2317.87
30/06/2013	2317.87		260.83	2057.04
30/06/2014	2057.04		231.48	1825.57

Depreciation:

30/6/2011	Depreciation	88.23	
	Accumulated depreciation lathe		88.23

Being: depreciation for 2011

30/6/2012	Depreciation	293.90	
	Accumulated depreciation lathe		293.90

Being: depreciation for 2012

30/6/2013 Depreciation   260.83

                Accumulated depreciation   260.83
                lathe

Being: depreciation for 2013

30/6/2014 Depreciation   231.48

                Accumulated depreciation   231.48
                lathe

Being: depreciation for 2014

Disposal:

01/11/2014 Cash at bank   3630.00

                Disposal of lathe   1980

                GST   198

                Private use   1452

Being: disposal proceeds of the lathe

Disposal of an asset		
Asset	Wood-working lathe	
Cost	$2700.00	
Effective life	13.33	
Depreciation rate	11.25%	
Date of last financial year	30/06/2014	
Closing balance	$1825.57	
Date of disposal	1/11/2014	
Disposal (termination) value	$1980.00	3630 × 10/11 × 60%
Depreciation adjustment	69.79	
Profit (loss) on disposal	$224.23	

01/11/2014 Depreciation   69.79

                  Accumulated depreciation   69.79
                  lathe

Being: residual depreciation on sale

01/11/2014 Disposal of lathe   2700.00

                  Wood-working lathe   2700.00

Being: cost of lathe to disposal account

01/11/2014 Accumulated depreciation   944.23
                  lathe

                  Disposal of lathe   944.23

Being: accumulated depreciation to disposal account

01/11/2014 Disposal of lathe   224.23

                  Profit on sale of asset   224.23

Being: profit transferred to other income account

Wood-working lathe — accumulated depreciation   **1515**

Date	Particulars	Folio	Debit	Credit	Balance
30/6/2011	Depreciation	GJ_N		88.23	(88.23)
30/6/2012	Depreciation	GJ_N		293.90	(382.13)
30/6/2013	Depreciation	GJ_N		260.83	(642.96)
30/6/2014	Depreciation	GJ_N		231.48	(874.44)
01/11/2014	Depreciation	GJ_N		69.79	(944.23)
01/11/2014	Disposal	GJ_N	944.23		0.00

Wood-working lathe   **1510**

Date	Particulars	Folio	Debit	Credit	Balance
16/03/2011	Cash	GJ_N	2700.00		2700.00
01/11/2014	Disposal	GJ_N		2700.00	0.00

Disposal of wood-working lathe   **9910**

Date	Particulars	Folio	Debit	Credit	Balance
01/11/2014	Proceeds	GJ_N		1980.00	(1980.00)
01/11/2014	Lathe cost	GJ_N	2700.00		720.00
01/11/2014	Depreciation	GJ_N		944.23	(224.23)
01/11/2014	Profit on sale	GJ_N	224.23		0.00

Profit on sale of assets   **9010**

Date	Particulars	Folio	Debit	Credit	Balance
01/11/2014	Lathe	GJ_N		224.23	(224.23)

Day 3: Inventory

Under the periodic system:

Periodic inventory record

Date	In	Out	Balance
1/09/2011	16		16
2/09/2011	27		43
3/09/2011		40	3
3/09/2011	18		21
4/09/2011	14		35
5/09/2011	22		57
5/09/2011		50	729
6/09/2011	25		32
7/09/2011	12		44
8/09/2011		40	4

Journal entry to record the sale:

8/09/2011	Cash at bank	1672.00	
	Sales		1520.00
	GST		152.00

Under the perpetual system:

Perpetual inventory system

Date	In	In ($)	Out (gross)	Out (gross value $)	Out (detail)	Out ($)	Balance	Balance ($)
1/09/2011	16	26.00					16	416.00
2/09/2011	27	26.00					43	1118.00
3/09/2011			40	1040.00	40	26.00	3	78.00
3/09/2011	18	28.00					21	582.00
4/09/2011	14	28.00					35	974.00
5/09/2011	22	30.00					57	1634.00
5/09/2011			50	1424.00	3	26.00	54	1556.00
					32	28.00	22	660.00
					15	30.00	7	210.00
6/09/2011	25	31.00					32	985.00
7/09/2011	12	31.50					44	1363.00
8/09/2011			40	1237.00	7	30.00	37	1153.00
					25	31.00	12	378.00
					8	31.50	4	126.00

Journal entry to record the sale:

8/09/2011	Cash at bank	1672.00	
	Sales		1520.00
	GST		152.00
8/09/2011	Cost of goods sold	1237.00	
	Inventory		1237.00

Day 4: End of year

Adjustments required:

Opening stock	28887	
Inventory		28887

Transfer the inventory asset to the CoS opening stock account:

Inventory	35897	
Closing stock		35897

Create the new closing inventory balance as both an asset and CoS:

Depreciation expense	7200	
Accumulated depreciation car		2700
Accumulated depreciation truck		4200
Accumulated depreciation trailer		300

Being: depreciation expense for the year

Rental income	1400	
Income in advance		1400

Being: rent paid in advance

Prepayments	3900	
Insurance		3900

Being: insurance paid in advance

Staff wages	2312	
Accrued expenses		2312

Being: wages owing but not yet paid

Staff leave	23 483	
Provision for leave		23 483

Being: accumulated leave balances

Income statement for the period ended 30 June YY

Revenue

Sales	459 234	
Less returns	1 245	457 989
Rent income	8 400	466 389

Less cost of sales

Opening inventory	28 887	
Plus purchases	162 562	
Inwards freight	35 123	
Goods available for sale	226 572	
Less closing stock	35 897	190 675
Trading or gross profit		275 714

Less expenses

Advertising	5 678	
Depreciation	7 200	
Electricity	13 874	
Insurance	14 100	
Rent	12 500	
Staff leave	46 290	
Staff wages	135 198	234 840
Net profit		**40 874**

Balance sheet as at 30 June YY

Assets

Current assets

Bank account	35 009		
Inventory	35 897		
Accounts receivable	3 225		
Prepaid expenses	3 900		78 031

Noncurrent assets

Car	25 000		
Less acc. depreciation	20 700	4300	
Truck	68 000		
Less acc. depreciation	43 700	24 300	
Trailer	12 000		
Less acc. depreciation	11 400	600	29 200
Total assets			**107 231**

Liabilities			
Current liability			
Income in advance	1 400		
Accrued expenses	2 312		
Provision for leave	23 483		27 195
Noncurrent liability			
Business loan			52 678
Equity			
Capital		12 000	
Retained earnings	50 858		
Less drawings	35 500	15 358	27 358
Total liabilities			**107 231**

Day 5: Cash and controls

Date	#	Details	In	Out	Balance	GST	Staff	Stationery	MV	Other
1 May			300.00		300.00					
2	1	Taxi		27.50	272.50	Y				27.50
3	2	Stationery		33.00	239.50	Y		33.00		
4	3	Private		68.00	171.50	N				68.00
5	4	Coffee		6.60	164.90	Y	6.60			
6	5	Newspapers		2.20	162.70	Y				2.20
7	6	Petrol		48.40	114.30	Y			48.40	
8		Reimburse	185.70		300.00		6.60	33.00	48.40	97.70

Date	Particulars	Folio	Debit	Credit
8 May	Staff amenities	6-5670	6.00	
	Stationery	6-4560	30.00	
	Motor vehicle	6-3500	44.00	
	Miscellaneous	6-9000	27.00	
	Drawings (fine)	3-2000	68.00	
	GST	2-9900	10.70	
	Cash	1-1000		185.70
	Being: petty cash reimbursement			

Note: the parking fine is not a legitimate business deduction. Although such expenditure can and often is paid through the petty cash system, when you do the reimbursement you must take these items into account when making up the journal entry.

Day 6: Employing and paying staff

Big Daddy Electrical Contractors
22 Fairfield Crescent, Nowhere NSW 2789
ABN 1234 12345

Pay date	2/06/2011	
Employee	Tom Smith	
Pay period	16/05/2011 to 1/06/2011	
Wages		
Wages	80 @ $45.00	3600.00
Allowances		
Tool		100.00
Travel	345k at $0.60	207.00
Deductions		
Income tax		924.00
Union	ETU	35.00
Amount paid		**$2948.00**
Superannuation guarantee to MySuper		**$324.00**

Big Daddy Electrical Contractors
22 Fairfield Crescent, Nowhere NSW 2789
ABN 1234 12345

Pay date	15/06/2011	
Employee	Tom Smith	
Pay period	2/06/2011 to 14/06/2011	

Wages		
Wages	80 @ $45.00	3600.00
Allowances		
Tool		100.00
Travel	245k at $0.60	147.00
Deductions		
Income tax		924.00
Union	ETU	35.00
Amount paid		**$2888.00**
Superannuation guarantee to MySuper		**$324.00**

Big Daddy Electrical Contractors
22 Fairfield Crescent, Nowhere NSW 2789
ABN 1234 12345

Pay date	29/06/2011	
Employee	Tom Smith	
Pay period	15/06/2011 to 28/06/2011	

Wages		
Wages	80 @ $45.00	3600.00
Overtime	8 @ 1.5	540.00
Allowances		
Tool		100.00
Travel	290k at $0.60	174.00
Deductions		
Income tax		1132.00
Union	ETU	35.00
Amount paid		**$3247.00**
Superannuation guarantee to MySuper		**$324.00**

Big Daddy Electrical Contractors		
22 Fairfield Crescent, Nowhere NSW 2789		
ABN 1234 12345		

Pay date	2/06/2011	
Employee	Richard Little	
Pay period	16/05/2011 to 1/06/2011	

Wages		
Wages	80 @ $25.00	2000.00
Overtime	8 @ 1.5	300.00
Allowances		
Tool		100.00
Travel	456k at $0.60	273.60
Deductions		
Income tax		472.00
Union	ETU	35.00
Amount paid		**$2166.60**
Superannuation guarantee to MySuper		**$180.00**

Big Daddy Electrical Contractors		
22 Fairfield Crescent, Nowhere NSW 2789		
ABN 1234 12345		

Pay date	15/06/2011	
Employee	Richard Little	
Pay period	2/06/2011 to 14/06/2011	

Wages		
Wages	80 @ $25.00	2000.00
Allowances		
Tool		100.00
Travel	214k at $0.60	128.40
Deductions		
Income tax		372.00
Union	ETU	35.00
Amount paid		**$1821.40**
Superannuation guarantee to MySuper		**$180.00**

Big Daddy Electrical Contractors
22 Fairfield Crescent, Nowhere NSW 2789
ABN 1234 12345

Pay date	29/06/2011	
Employee	Richard Little	
Pay period	15/06/2011 to 28/06/2011	
Wages		
Wages	80 @ $25.00	2000.00
Allowances		
Tool		100.00
Travel	314k at $0.60	188.40
Deductions		
Income tax		372.00
Union	ETU	35.00
Amount paid		**$1881.40**
Superannuation guarantee to MySuper		**$180.00**

Payment summary as at 30/6/11 — calculation sheet

Date	Wages	Overtime	Tool	Travel	Income tax	Union	Net
Tom							
2/06/2011	3 600.00		100.00	207.00	924.00	35.00	2948.00
15/06/2011	3 600.00		100.00	147.00	924.00	35.00	2888.00
29/06/2011	3 600.00	540.00	100.00	174.00	1132.00	35.00	3247.00
	10 800.00	**540.00**	**300.00**	**528.00**	**2980.00**	**105.00**	**9083.00**
		11 340.00		*828.00*			
Richard							
2/06/2011	2 000.00	300.00	100.00	273.60	472.00	35.00	2166.60
15/06/2011	2 000.00		100.00	128.40	372.00	35.00	1821.40
29/06/2011	2 000.00		100.00	188.40	372.00	35.00	1881.40
	6 000.00	**300.00**	**300.00**	**590.40**	**1216.00**	**105.00**	**5869.40**
		6 300.00		*890.40*			

PAYG payment summary

Section A	Payee details
Payee surname	Smith
Payee given name	Tom
Payee address	125 Anywhere Street Nowhere NSW 3456
Date of birth	16/10/75
Section B	**Payment details**
Period	01/07/2010 to 30/06/2011
Payee TFN	783478912
Total tax withheld	2980 *two thousand nine hundred and eighty*
Gross payments	11 340
Allowances	Tool 300 Travel 528
Union dues	Electrical Trades Union 105
Section C	**Payer details**
Payer's ABN	1234 12345
Payer's name	Big Daddy Electrical Contractors

PAYG payment summary

Section A	Payee details
Payee surname	Little
Payee given name	Richard
Payee address	128 Anywhere Street Nowhere NSW 3456
Date of birth	16/4/1989
Section B	**Payment details**
Period	01/07/2010 to 30/06/2011
Payee TFN	34528512
Total tax withheld	1216 *twelve hundred and sixteen*
Gross payments	6300

Allowances	Tool	300
	Travel	590
Union dues	Electrical Trades Union	105

Section C	**Payer details**
Payer's ABN	1234 12345
Payer's name	Big Daddy Electrical Contractors

Day 7: Taxation of unused leave entitlements on termination

Tom works an 80 hour fortnight at $45 per hour, equating to $3600 per pay fortnight. His leave balance on termination was 20.5 hours at $45 per hour. This equates to $922.50.

▶ Calculate the tax in the normal way but only on the 'normal' gross income without the unused leave balances included:

$$80 \text{ hours @ } \$45 = \$3600$$

$$\text{Tax on } \$3600 \text{ per fortnight} = \$924.00$$

▶ Calculate the amount of unused leave payments, in this case $922.50, and divide that number by the number of pay periods in the year, in our case 26:

$$\$922.50/26 = \$35.48$$

▶ Add the normal gross income to the 1/26th of the leave payment:

$$\$3600 + \$35.48 = \$3635.48$$

▶ Now work out the tax on this elevated figure using the TWC calculator:

$$\$938.00$$

▶ The final calculation is to work out the difference between the two tax amounts:

$$\$924 - \$938 = \$14.$$

Multiply that difference by 26:

$$\$14 \times 26 = \$364.$$

So $364 is the tax payable on the unused leave balance paid on termination of employment.

Appendix D
Glossary

accounting   the process of systematically recording, analysing and interpreting transactions.

accounting entity   for accounting purposes, all businesses are considered to be separate entities from their owners. This means that the accounting records of the business must be kept separate from the owner's records. See also *legal entity*.

accounting equation   the relationship between the balance sheet items, usually expressed as assets = liabilities + equity. Also known as the balance sheet equation, it forms the basis of the layout for the balance sheet.

accounting period   a period of one year, usually between 1 July and 30 June. This is distinct from the bookkeeping cycle that is based on the calendar month.

accounting process   the systematic procedure for recording business transactions. See also *bookkeeping*.

accounting standards   International Financial Reporting Standards (IFRS) as accepted by the Australian Accounting

Standards Board. Usually these standards only apply to large or medium enterprises reporting to third parties, such as shareholders. See also *Tax Office standards*.

accounts payable   a *general ledger* account that holds the total amount that we owe to our suppliers for inventory purchased on credit terms; also known as *trade payables* or *creditors control*. The individual accounts for each supplier are held in the creditors subsidiary ledger.

accounts receivable   a *general ledger* account that holds the total amount that we are owed by our customers who have purchased inventory from us on credit terms; also known as *trade receivables* or *debtors control*. The individual accounts for each customer are held in the debtors subsidiary ledger.

accrual accounting   all transactions are recorded when the contract is made, not when the amounts are settled. This is irrespective of whether or not it was a cash transaction and irrespective of the fact that the *GST* is creditable or due when the transaction is recorded. This can lead to cash flow problems for small businesses.

adjustment note   a credit note issued by the supplier of goods or services, adjusting (usually reducing) the amount outstanding and also proportionally adjusting the *GST* component of the transaction.

annual leave   the amount of leave accumulated by an employee to be taken as a paid holiday, usually 20 working days per full time employee, pro rated for part time employees.

assets   items of value owned by the business and used by the business to earn revenue.

Australian business number (ABN)   the business identifier allocated by the ATO. All businesses should register for an ABN even though they may not be required to register for the *GST*.

Australian Taxation Office (ATO) the government's principal revenue collection agency.

bad debts credit customers who fail to pay their full debt on time and with little likelihood of recovery.

balance day the last day of the accounting period, usually 30 June.

balance sheet a document showing in detail the assets, liabilities and owner's equity items at a particular time; shows the financial position of the business at this date.

bank reconciliation statement a report itemising the differences between the cash records of the business and those of the bank. After taking into account *unpresented cheques* and *unrecorded deposits*, the two records should agree.

bank statement a document prepared by the bank listing customers' use of their cheque accounts—for example, each deposit, presented cheque and automatic transfer.

bookkeeping the systematic recording of transactions by documents, journals and ledgers.

bookkeeping period the monthly cycle of data entry, verification and report (trial balance and BAS).

book value the historical cost of an asset (what you paid for it) less any accumulated depreciation.

borrowing costs the costs associated with the borrowing of money, but not including interest, such as the legal cost of writing up the mortgage contract. These are usually recorded as an expense under accounting standards and as an asset under the tax rules to be amortised over five years (or the length of the loan contract if shorter).

business activity statement (BAS) the return that all businesses must lodge with the *ATO* monthly, quarterly or annually. It incorporates the *GST* return and records such tax liabilities as pay-as-you-go (PAYG) withholding, PAYG income tax and fringe benefits tax (FBT).

capital   the value of the owner's investment in the business.

capitalised costs   an outlay of money that is recorded as an asset and then written off as an expense over time, usually in the form of depreciation.

cash   not only means actual money, but in business usually means cheques and also includes direct debits and credit card transactions.

cash accounting   under *ATO* rules this is more accurately modified cash accounting; that is, all assets and liabilities are recorded when the contract is made, irrespective of when the cash changes hands. However, for income and expense items, they are only recorded when you settle the account, irrespective of whether it was a cash or credit transaction.

cash at bank (CAB)   money (cash, cheques, money orders, credit card sales and direct debits) deposited in the cheque account. All cash receipts should be banked intact and recorded in the cash receipts journal. All payments should be made by cheque or electronically (but never by cash) and recorded in the cash payments journal.

chart of accounts   a list of all the *general ledger* accounts coded and in order, a numerical index to the general ledger accounts.

company   a business owned by a shareholder or shareholders; a separate *legal entity* from its owners.

consignment   when goods are sent on consignment, the consignor retains ownership while the goods are waiting to be sold. The consignee stores the goods and presents them for sale. At the time of sale, ownership passes to the buyer; at no time does the consignee own the goods.

consumer a person who purchases a product or service for personal use; the last link in the distribution chain.

control account a *general ledger* account that summarises many transactions recorded in a subsidiary ledger. For example, the *creditors control* holds the monthly totals of the amounts posted to the creditors ledger and its balance is the balance outstanding of all creditors in the individual creditors accounts.

cost of sales often referred to as COGS, this ledger classification holds the cost of inventory purchases, plus inwards freight, customs duties and any other costs incurred in getting your goods for resale delivered to your back door. When determining the annual profit, the COGS is adjusted to account for the movement in the inventory over the year.

credit an entry in a *general ledger* account that represents the economic outflows from a business transaction.

creditors account see *accounts payable*.

creditors control see *accounts payable*.

credit purchase a purchase of trading stock on credit terms; for example, 'Net 14 days'.

credit sale the sale of trading stock on credit terms.

current assets cash or other assets (such as *trading stock* or *trade debtors*) that are convertible to cash within one year.

current liabilities debts or other financial obligations payable within one year (such as *trade creditors*).

debit an entry in a *general ledger* account that represents the economic inflows from a business transaction.

debtors account see *accounts receivable*.

debtors control see *accounts receivable*.

decline in value *ATO* term used for *depreciation*. The rate of depreciation is determined by accounting standards whereas the decline in value is a tax deductible amount determined by the ATO. Most *micro businesses* use the ATO decline in value amounts as their depreciable amounts.

depreciation the annual allocation of part of an asset's historical cost to an expense in recognition of its depleting value over time; see also *decline in value*.

dishonoured cheque a cheque presented to the bank but unable to be honoured, usually due to insufficient cash in the drawer's bank account.

double-entry bookkeeping the basic principle of recording the economic flow of business transactions—for every debit entry (economic flow inwards) there must be an equivalent credit entry (economic flow outwards) in the *general ledger*.

drawings cash, stock or anything else of value that the owner takes out of the business for personal use.

final reports the end-of-period reports, balance sheet, income statement and cash flow statement

franchise a business arrangement where, for an initial fee and usually an annual payment, a business may operate using a trademark or trade name and use knowledge and expertise provided by the franchisor.

general journal a journal used to record transactions for which a special journal is not suitable; see also *special journal*.

general ledger a collection of ledger accounts into which transactions are posted in total from journals; holds the details of business transactions of the same type.

GST (goods and services tax) a tax on goods and services sold within Australia. The tax is collected by the provider of the good or service and remitted to the *ATO* on a *BAS* form on a quarterly basis, net of any GST paid on purchases made by the provider.

GST free   supplies, goods or services that are *GST* exempt, such as basic foodstuffs.

HELP (Higher Education Loan Program)   government support for tertiary students that is repaid through their taxable earnings. Previously known as Higher Education Contribution Scheme (HECS).

imprest system   usually associated with petty cash, a system whereby a float is advanced from which expenses are paid and a periodic reimbursement made. The cash on hand plus the expense vouchers must always equal the original float amount.

income statement   a document showing the revenues earned by a business and expenses incurred. Expenses are subtracted from revenues, leaving a net profit or loss. Also called a profit and loss statement or a *statement of financial performance* (IFRS).

incurred   with regard to a business transaction, it is the time that the contract became binding and an amount of money is due, either now or in the future. It is at this point that transactions are normally recorded in your accounting records; for cash-based businesses this recording time is delayed until the account is actually settled.

input tax credit   *GST* paid by a 'registered' purchaser on which the purchaser can claim a tax credit on their *BAS*.

internal control   a set of systems and procedures put in place by a business to safeguard its assets and ensure reliability of its accounting information.

International Financial Reporting Standards (IFRS)   see *accounting standards* and *Tax Office standards*.

inventory   the goods you purchase for resale at a profit. The purchase of inventory is debited to the purchases account under COGS. The cost of inventory in your accounts is determined by your annual stocktake. See also *cost of sales*.

journal   a summary of transactions that are first evidenced by business 'source' documents. The details on these documents are transferred to journals, such as the *general journal,* cash receipts journal, cash payments journal, purchases journal and sales journal, on a periodic, often daily, basis. The journals are totalled monthly and posted to the *general ledger*.

ledger account   a record of each individual type of account, for example, an electricity account or a motor vehicle account.

legal entity   a legal concept identifying the possessor of legal rights and obligations, such as the ability to make contracts in its own name, obligation to pay debts or taxes, ability to initiate legal proceedings or be sued. As a contrast, see *accounting entity*.

long service leave   an employee's entitlement to an amount of accumulated leave, usually three months after 15 years of service. Usually paid pro rata after 10 years.

Medicare levy   an additional tax on your net income of 1.5 per cent payable after a minimum earnings level has been met.

micro business   see *small business*.

net profit (loss)   the difference between revenue earned and expenses incurred; profit (loss) = revenue less expenses.

net wage   an amount paid to an employee after all deductions, including income tax, have been made.

noncurrent assets   items of value that will not be exchanged for or converted to cash within the next 12 months, such as your business premises or motor vehicles.

noncurrent liabilities obligations that do not require payment within the next 12 months, such as a mortgage.

operating cycle the continuous flow of business transactions. Cash from sales comes into the business and is used to pay suppliers and other business expenses and buy more stock. When sold, the stock generates cash and so the cycle continues.

ordinary time earnings (OTE) what employees earn for their ordinary hours of work including over-award payments, bonuses, commissions, allowances and certain paid leave.

overdraft a loan from a financial institution made available through the cheque (trading) account. The business can continue to write cheques even though there are insufficient funds in the bank to cover them, up to an agreed value.

owner's equity the accounts classification that in total shows the net worth of the owner's investment in the business, often referred to as proprietorship.

partnership a business owned by two to 20 persons, each of whom is bound by the others' decisions and liable for all the debts of the business *(unlimited liability)*. Partnership structures are governed by the various state Partnership Acts.

partnership agreement a contract between partners of a business documenting each partner's rights, duties and liabilities.

payroll deductions amounts deducted from an employee's gross income. May be voluntary, such as union dues, or compulsory, such as income tax.

petty cash a small amount of cash on hand used to pay minor expenses, such as milk for the canteen.

posting the transferring of journal totals to the *general ledger* accounts.

profit and loss statement more correctly known as an *income statement* or a *statement of financial performance*.

proprietary company a 'private' company registered with Australian Securities and Investments Commission (ASIC) owned by a shareholder or shareholders (maximum 50), with the words 'Proprietary Limited' (Pty Ltd) after its name.

public company usually a large company with the word 'Limited' (Ltd) after the name. It has the right to offer shares to the public at large and has no restrictions on the transfer of shares.

purchase order a document requesting a supplier to deliver specified items at a specified price; it is an offer to purchase, not a contract.

purchases expenses incurred in buying and trading stock for cash or on credit; in a cash-based business the purchase is recorded when the goods are actually paid for and not when the expense is incurred.

reportable fringe benefits if an employer provides to an employee fringe benefits with a taxable value of more than $2000 in a year, the employer must report the grossed-up taxable value of the benefits on the employee's payment summary.

revenue money earned by a business. Trading businesses earn revenue from selling and trading stock, and service businesses by providing knowledge and skills for a fee.

revenue earned *revenue* that a business can legally record as revenue even though cash has not been received because a contract of sale has been concluded. Revenue is normally recognised when earned, not when received, but in cash-based businesses it is only recognised on receipt.

salary an amount paid to an employee as a fixed remuneration. Salaried employees are usually not entitled to overtime payments.

sales revenue   income earned from selling and trading stock for cash or credit.

service business   a business providing specialised knowledge and skills, such as medical, gardening or accounting businesses. Income earned is from fees.

sick or personal leave   an amount accumulated by an employee to be used for sickness or other personal reasons. Usually not paid out on termination of employment.

small business   the generally accepted term for businesses with a turnover between $2 million and $20 million and fewer than five employees.

small business entity   a tax term for a business with a turnover of less than $2 million.

small to medium enterprise (SME)   business entities that usually fall within the $20 million to $100 million turnover that are subject to IFRS.

sole trader   a business owned by one person who is liable for all debts of the business *(unlimited liability)*.

special journals   journals summarising one type of transaction; for example, the sales journal summarises credit sales of trading stock.

statement of cash flows   shows the source of cash used by the business, and the use to which that cash was put. The cash flow statement is the third member of the trilogy comprising balance sheet, income statement and cash flow statement.

statement of financial performance   alternative name for the *income statement* as defined under IFRS.

statement of financial position   alternative name for *balance sheet* as defined under IFRS.

stock   the items a trading business buys and sells (trades in); also referred to as goods or trading stock. See also *inventory*.

stock in trade   see *inventory*.

subsidiary ledger   a ledger providing detail to support the *general ledger;* commonly used for *trade debtors, trade creditors, stock* and payroll. The *general ledger* includes summary accounts called control accounts, while the subsidiary ledgers record the full details for each debtor, creditor, stock item or employee.

sundry creditor   a person or business to whom the business owes money as a result of purchasing an asset, such as a motor vehicle, other than trading stock on credit.

superannuation guarantee contributions   the minimum amount of employer superannuation contributions an employer must make for an employee.

T account   a pre-computerisation ledger format where the left side of the 'T' records debit entries and the right records credit entries.

tax-free threshold   an amount of income not subject to income tax. Usually applies only to Australian tax residents.

Tax Office standards   the Income Tax Assessment Acts contain a number of concessionary rules in regard to *small businesses*. The Commissioner of Taxation, usually referred to as the Tax Office or the *ATO,* has issued a number of publications on the interpretation and application of these rules. It is by these rules, rather than the *IFRS,* that most small businesses abide. See also *accounting standards*.

termination payment   an amount paid to an employee as a result of termination of their employment. May include accrued leave entitlements.

trade creditor   a person or business to which the business owes money for services or stock purchased on credit; see also *accounts payable*.

trade debtor   a person or business that owes the business money for services or stock sold on credit; see also *accounts receivable*.

trade payables   see *accounts payable*.

trade receivables   see *accounts receivable*.

trading business   a business that buys and sells trading stock (includes retailers and *wholesalers*).

trading name   the name your business can trade under (provided that you have registered it with the appropriate state authority).

trading stock   see *inventory*.

transaction   the exchange of goods or services that results in an obligation to pay or receive money.

trial balance   a list of *general ledger* account balances; checks that debit balances equal credit balances.

turnover   used as in small business turnover under $2 million; includes all ordinary income you earn in the ordinary course of business for the income year.

unlimited liability   an obligation to pay business debts that is not limited to the value of business assets or the ownership percentage of the business and extends to the personal assets of investors.

unpresented cheques   cheques that have been written by the business and sent to creditors, but have not been deposited into a bank account (presented) by the time the *bank statement* has been prepared.

unrecorded deposits deposits recorded in the business records but not recorded by the bank at the time the *bank statement* was prepared.

wage an amount paid to an employee based upon the number of hours worked. Wage employees are usually entitled to overtime payments and shift allowances.

wholesaler a business that purchases stock from manufacturers or their representatives and on-sells them to retailers (the middle man).

Index

Also in the Learn in 7 Days series

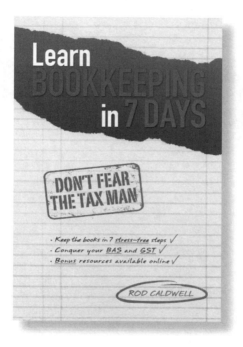

Available from all good bookstores